I'll Meet You at the Northeast Corner of... Heaven

A Story of Discovery, Love, and The Choices We Make

Barbara Butler Norrell
with Paula R. Bryant

I'll Meet You at The Northeast Corner of Heaven
A Story of Discovery, Love, and The Choices We Make
By Barbara Butler Norrell with Paula R. Bryant

Unless otherwise noted, all Scripture quotations are taken from The New American Standard Bible (NAS). Copyright © 1960, 1962, 1963, 1968, 1971, 1972, 1973, 1975, 1977, by The Lockman Foundation. Used by permission. All rights reserved.

Scripture references marked (NIV) are taken from THE HOLY BIBLE: NEW INTERNATIONAL VERSION (r). NIV (r). Copyright © 1973, 1978, 1984 by International Bible Society. Used by permission of Zondervan Publishing House. All rights reserved.

Scripture references marked (NKJ) are taken from The New King James Version, copyright (c) 1982, Thomas Nelson, Inc. All rights reserved.

Scripture references marked (TLB) are taken from The Living Bible, copyright (c) 1971. Used by permission of Tyndale House Publishers, Inc., Wheaton, IL 60189. All rights reserved.

Scripture references marked (Ampl.) are taken from THE AMPLIFIED BIBLE, Copyright © 1954, 1958, 1962, 1964, 1965, 1987 by The Lockman Foundation. All rights reserved. Used by permission. (www.Lockman.org)

Scripture references marked (RSV) are taken from the Revised Standard Version of the Bible, copyright (c) 1946, 1952, 1971 by the Division of Christian Education of the National Council of the Churches of Christ in the USA, and is used by permission.

Scripture references marked (KJV) are taken from The King James Version, *PC Study Bible*. Biblesoft. © 1993–1998. All rights reserved.

Scripture references marked (LAB) are taken from the Life Application Study Bible, New International Version, Tyndale House Publishers, Inc. and Zondervan Publishing House, Wheaton, IL and Grand Rapids, MI. Copyright © 1988, 1989, 1990, 1991. All rights reserved.

Cover Design by ASarah Publications C E S

Copyright © 2003 by Barbara Butler Norrell
ISBN 0-9740865-0-9
Library of Congress Control Number: 2003104335

This book or parts thereof may not be reproduced in any form, stored in a retrieval system, or transmitted in any form by any means—electronic, mechanical, photocopy, recording, or otherwise—without prior written permission of the publisher, except as provided by United States of America copyright law.

Why You Should Join The Journey...

It takes a "good book" to keep my attention.
> I found the story so interesting; I didn't want to put it down! This morning, I woke up at 5:00...and all I could think about was getting back to the manuscript while everyone was asleep and my household was quiet. WOW!! What a story to tell! It was so clear that God was with her, every step of the journey, even when she wasn't aware of His almighty presence. It inspired me to pray more for God's will in my life. Hopefully, this is the first of many books to come...
> • Mrs. L. Phillips

Excellent and to the point...
> This is a book that many have tried to produce and have been unsuccessful due to capacity. Barb has filled the pages with a warm story of love, hope, and faith. We will all benefit from her story.
> • Ms. E. Mitchell

This is a frank, honest, and fascinating book.
> Barbara has shielded us from nothing as she takes us through the odyssey of her life of promise, addiction, and redemption. It graphically shows that God is a God of second chances, and that even after we have thoroughly messed things up, He still loves us enough to take what's left and make it beautiful again. Careful...there's a risk you'll open yourself up as much as Barb does.
> • Dr. N. Weaver

Relevant advice for all women...
> • Ms. M. Todd

Out of Barb's honesty came a book about events and relationships.
> It's a very clear picture of how we all fall short of the glory of God, and how God forgives and repairs our lives.
> • Mrs. M. Brady

The detailed, graphic, and intimate references were revealing.
> Faith was growing, maturity was developing...
> • Dr. H. Ritchie

To Larry, my hero.

To my church, family, and friends...especially the *Reel to Real* women who have faithfully committed themselves to my vision. I am truly blessed by each of you. *And to eight special people* who took their time to review this manuscript early on. I'm enlightened by your insight and wisdom, and encouraged by your words.
Thank you. Thank you.

Contents

Introduction — xi

Part I A Place Called "Here"

Chapter 1   Me, Me, Me — 17
The Preliminaries: From Dating To Marriage

Chapter 2   There's More To Follow — 29
Growing in Love: The Struggle To Conceive

Chapter 3   Oh Lukey Bob, Oh Lukey Bob — 43
Enduring Love: Our Unexpected Miracle

Chapter 4   Can't You Understand, I Want To Be A Mom? — 57
Labors of Love: Discovering What Matters Most

Chapter 5   Hey, I Didn't Marry A Pastor! — 73
Guiding Love: Helping Others To Find The Way

Chapter 6   The Taste of The Pear — 85
True Love: Seeing through Each Other's Eyes

Part II A Place Called "There"

Chapter 7   I'm Outta Here! — 97
Frustrated Love: Escaping The Ideal Family

Chapter 8   Oh Happy Day — 113
Misdirected Love: A Journey in Self Discovery

Chapter 9   Houston, We Have A Problem — 123
When Love Is Lost: Starting Over Again

Chapter 10   Living The High Life — 137
Self Love: The Hardest Lesson

Chapter 11   Know It? I Wrote It. — 153
Perfect Love: Resting in God

Part III Things I've Learned "Here" and "There"

Chapter 12   What Dreams Are Made Of — 167
Life Lessons on Attitude, Family, Money, Weight & More

Introduction

Soon after the terrorist tragedy of September 11, 2001 (i.e., the bombing of the World Trade Center in New York City), my husband Larry walked into the kitchen as I was preparing breakfast for our son. He said, "You know, Barb, if this world should end today, I'll meet you and Luke at the northeast corner of heaven." My first response was, "What?" After he repeated himself, I asked, "Could you be more specific?" Then Larry said, "Well how specific is that? It's a one-foot space at the corner. I'll meet you there, okay?" I agreed, and he walked out the door on his way to work.

Larry's heavenly invitation inspired me to write this book; it gave me a new perspective in these uncertain times and reminded me that no matter what happens in the world around us, our family has an awesome future in eternity with the Lord. We simply have to keep focused on heaven as we live each day on earth.

This book is about love. It's my story. A story about the love I have for my husband. A story about the love I have for my young child. And a story about the love I've come to know for my most gracious heavenly Father. I don't take love for granted, not after the things I've come through to gain the understanding I have today. Oh, what a wonderful feeling it is to be sure I'm going to heaven and that my family will be there, too.

Life Has Many Layers

All in all, I've come to realize the *journey* of life is most important—so that's how I arranged this book. There are three parts: The first deals with my life now, after accepting Christ as my Savior

And which of you by being anxious can add a {single} cubit to his life's span?
Matt. 6:27

Do not be anxious then, saying, What shall we eat? or What shall we drink? or With what shall we clothe ourselves?
Matt. 6:31

But seek first His kingdom and His righteousness; and all these things shall be added to you.
Matt. 6:33

(because this has given me a new perspective about things in my past). The second part deals with my life before I came to know the Lord, and the third section is a topical discussion of things I've learned along the way.

Each one of us makes choices every moment of every day; this forms the basis of what we experience in life. When we reach our final destination (and I hope it will be heaven for you, as well), we'll look back on the marks we've made during our journeys. *Like an onion, our lives have many layers.* Some are good, and some aren't so good. We must learn to peel back the layers, throwing away the bad ones and using what's good. It's absolutely our choice. Every day, we must uncover the areas that need work and rediscover the positive aspects of life.

Maybe you or someone you know will read my story and relate to the many twists and turns my life has taken, bringing me to where I am today (I've changed some names here and there for privacy reasons). *Like an onion, my life had layers that needed revealing.* Some were sweet, and some brought tears—but most importantly, God graciously used each layer to establish and perfect His principle of love in my life. I'm forever grateful.

At the end of each chapter, you'll find *Reflection* questions based on what I've shared from my experiences. They'll give you an opportunity to reflect on your own life, and perhaps pull back hidden layers of hurt, pain, insecurities, low self-esteem, unworthiness, abandonment, mistrust, and a flood of many different emotions. Make sure you have a journal handy (or simply a pen and paper) as you read, because if you take a little time to look honestly at your life, you're going to gain a fresh outlook.

It All Boils Down To Love

In the wake of numerous reality television shows, I'm always amazed at what people will do for love. Everyone seems to be looking for his or her fairytale to come true. It's such a fascination! I searched for love all of my life, and made a lot of mistakes in the process—but now I know that love is real. And I've learned that fairytales can come true...if you want them badly enough.

My hope and prayer is that you'll find true joy and happiness in your life. I pray that after reading my story, you'll walk away with a new perspective that will lead you to victory time and time again. It's never too late to change, and it's entirely possible to have a sense of inner peace and contentment (especially in today's world). It all begins with a personal relationship with our Lord, Jesus Christ.

Larry has often said people need three homes. We need a home here on earth, we need a church home, and we need a heavenly home. I couldn't agree more...because home is where the heart is. And the heart is the place Jesus enters our lives, *because that's where love is born*.

I once heard the greatest thing you'll ever learn is to love and be loved in return. May you find your place of peace on earth. And when you reach heaven, pick your corner.

Enjoy...and may God bless you.

Part I

A Place Called "Here"

But seek first His kingdom and His righteousness; and all these things shall be added to you. Therefore do not be anxious for tomorrow; for tomorrow will care for itself. {Each} day has enough trouble of its own.

Matthew 6:33–34

Chapter 1

Me, Me, Me

The Preliminaries: From Dating To Marriage

People were always trying to set me up with the "perfect" man. It seemed I was everyone's definition of a great candidate—young, attractive, and successful in my career. And I was on my way to yet another "arranged" date. A blind date. Out of town. Somebody a friend told me that I just had to meet.

As I drove to the airport pondering where I was going to stay that night (there were no return flights until the next day), I couldn't stop thinking about Larry. We had only dated twice for lunch, no big deal. Yet at that moment, while I was on my way to meet another man, I realized that I was falling in love with him. I squeezed the steering wheel (as though it would help me to keep it together! Ha!), but it was too late...I was definitely falling.

Larry entered my life at a time when I was getting tired of living the high life and pursuing empty relationships. Some were totally out of my control, others were due to my own bad decisions; but one way or another, they all tied into love (or the lack of it)—for myself, my family, and others. I'd made a lot of stupid mistakes, but was still determined to build a better future. At the time, I was thirty-four and had been single for eleven years after divorcing my high school sweetheart. I wasn't looking for a committed relationship, and I definitely wasn't walking with God (I'll get to this later).

Yet somehow, I knew there was more. I believed one day there would be a man for whom I could have the highest respect.

Someone that I'd love deeply, and he'd love me equally as much. And it happened, but it took time. In the meantime, though, my friends started trying to help me make things happen. I know they meant well. They just didn't understand why someone who appeared to be so happy, held a decent job, and had all the things she wanted wasn't married. They constantly asked, "Barb, when are you going to get married? Hasn't anyone asked you to marry him yet?"

For me, it was simple. I hadn't met the "prime pick," the man who would be my Prince Charming—*my perfect match*. No matter how old I was, or how many dates didn't pan out, I always believed there was something and someone better for me. And I was right.

Our Fairytale Beginning

Larry swept me off my feet. He was everything I wanted: big, tall, and handsome with a deep, commanding voice. I loved his strength. He had such a command about him, yet he was a real gentleman: thoughtful, considerate, and romantic in every way. He even wrote poems and had them delivered to me at work! What a guy!

Mostly, I loved Larry's eyes. They were blue or green, depending on his mood. Blue was his romantic color, the color that I saw most. Actually, I thought his eyes were only blue for a long time, until one day I looked at him and saw green. "Get 'em back to blue," I said. To this day, I love his romantic eyes.

Larry and I had a whirlwind romance. We met in 1994, and our first date was in mid-October. By December 5, he proposed, and we were married in Jamaica on December 29. It was like a dream come true. I knew I'd found my Prince Charming. Yet, every relationship takes work...and Larry seemed to know this from the very beginning. He never took our relationship lightly.

For our first dinner date, Larry took me on a wonderful carriage ride and then strummed a few love songs on his guitar. As I listened to him play and sing, *You Don't Know Me* and *Can't Help Falling In Love*, I remember thinking, "This is so corny...but I love it!" With every stroke of the guitar, I was melting. Larry won my heart. He was so incredibly masculine, yet so willing to do those sensitive things that touched me deeply. Oh yes, Larry knew how to build a life-long relationship.

On another memorable evening, Larry took me to see the movie, *A Love Affair* (a remake of *An Affair To Remember*, only this time starring Warren Beatty and Annette Bening). When they finally acknowledged their love at the end of the movie, my emotions erupted. I cried all the way from the theater to the car just thinking about it. In the midst of my sobs, Larry pulled off his T-shirt (it was a warm evening) and handed it to me to blow my nose! Then he looked deep into my eyes and said, "Let's get happy. Let me take you by the mall...I was just there the other day and saw this little shop I thought you'd like." That definitely made me happy!

When we arrived at the boutique, and as I glanced at the dresses displayed in the window, Larry said, "Would you like to try one on? I want to buy one for you." I looked at him in amazement thinking, "Is this guy for real? I'm really starting to like him..." Moments later, a saleswoman appeared with a few dresses—I was shocked to see a beautiful, white dress (with a matching hat) among the choices. And it was strikingly similar to a dress Annette Bening had worn in the movie! Beautiful and flowing, it looked great on me. I was stunned. Larry made the purchase.

I found out later that Larry had planned the entire evening, to the finest detail. He'd already seen the movie, visited the shop, picked out the dress, and arranged with the staff to bring it out when we arrived! Larry always surprised me with wonderful things. He pulled out all the stops to please me.

When Larry and I started dating, we lived in different cities. I lived in Dallas, Texas, and he lived a few hours away in San Antonio. I worked for an airline company, though, and could fly for free—so that wasn't a problem. I simply flew to San Antonio to see him. One night, however, I couldn't get a flight back; so he got a nice hotel room for me on the River Walk (a quaint, romantic stretch of river that runs through downtown San Antonio).

It was a wonderful evening. He took me to the hotel, and we sat on a ground floor veranda gazing at the river. (What I didn't know was he'd paid a bellman to run to my room, light candles everywhere, and have champagne waiting on ice.) I let Larry come to the room and visit a while, and then made him leave. After all, we were just getting to know each other! We met for breakfast the next morning at the hotel before I left.

I'll never forget these special times. Larry never ceased to amaze me. He always planned ahead to make things special, and is still the same. He's an excellent man and a wonderful husband.

From "Me" To "Us"

Larry and I love movies. Another one of our favorites is *Groundhog Day*, because for us, it's come to symbolize the process of how we became one in our marriage. (Believe it or not, we celebrate February 2 each year! It's a sentimental time for us.) Anyway, in one of the scenes, Andie McDowell tells Bill Murray she's looking for a man who's "...kind, sensitive, caring, and will change poopie diapers." After each point, Bill quips sarcastically, "Me, Me, Me..." Yet throughout the movie, he keeps trying to win her heart...and because he lives the same day over and over again, he finally succeeds.

In reality, no one has the ability to keep starting the same day over again just to get things right, but we do have the ability to change. It's human nature to want things for ourselves, to look out for number one. Yet we often fail to realize how selfish we are until someone we love brings it to light. Giving is the basis of love. If we don't give, our relationships won't survive. When we choose to give, our relationships come to life.

Before Larry and I married, I always looked out for number one—mostly due to unresolved issues from my childhood. *My life changed forever on our wedding night...*

It had been a beautiful day. We'd just gotten married in one of the most romantic places on earth—Jamaica—and had made a wedding video to share with our family. I remember saying to Larry during a filmed interview, "I'm so glad you're coming into my life because something is really missing..." Later, as I relaxed in his arms, I shared, "I'm so happy that I've met you. You make me happy, and I can see this happy life coming up...I don't want to die, Larry, life is so good! Do you ever think about death?"

Apparently, my comments really made an impression on him. Larry had once been a pastor and still believed deeply in God. When we met, though, I think he was trying to get some normalcy in his life. Men don't like being alone, and Larry needed someone to "complete" him. He'd been divorced and out of the ministry

> *It's human nature to want things for ourselves, to look out for number one. Yet we often fail to realize how selfish we are until someone we love brings it to light.*

for more than eight years, but he still knew there was more...and he knew "more" came only from our heavenly Father. When I think back, I believe what took place between us that night was Larry's first step back to his destiny—the call to pastor and preach.

Larry and I had never spoken about God, religion, or his desire to return to the pulpit before we were married. Maybe he was trying to forget the past. I know that I was trying to forget mine! Nevertheless, I believe God allowed us to meet for that reason. Neither one of us entered our marriage from a spiritual perspective, but God had a bigger plan.

When I asked Larry about death, I think it touched something he'd buried deep in his heart. So when he realized I was scared to die...he led me to Jesus. That night Larry led me in the prayer of salvation, and my life has never been the same. Not only did I gain a wonderful husband, I met my heavenly Father! I'm eternally grateful to Larry for telling me about the Lord.

This brings me back to *Groundhog Day* and, *Me, Me, Me*. Love cannot be complete until God, the Author of love, comes into your life. This is how we can truly care about the needs of others and put others first. In any relationship, it's easy to see the other person's faults and not our own. When you accept Jesus Christ as your savior, He begins to make you more like Him. That's when you start looking inside at what needs to change in you.

Years later, I was in a Sunday School class and the teacher asked us to go around the room and tell about when we were saved. My turn came, and I simply said, "I was saved on my wedding night." Peels of laughter filled the room, along with a few, "Hallelujahs!" but I was as serious as I could be. It was on my wedding

Love cannot be complete until God, the Author of love, comes into your life. This is how we can truly care about the needs of others and put others first.

day that I realized I was afraid to die...*because I felt as if my life was just beginning*.

Getting To Know You

Larry and I had a magical start, but everything had happened so quickly! We still had a lot to learn about each other. So here we were, newly married, yet each of us was about to begin a difficult journey of self-exploration. Our fairytale courtship actually set us up for great challenges later. In the beginning, it had been so romantic. So perfect. And our expectations of each other were so high that our first two years of marriage were a disaster. The day-to-day realities of married life proved to be much more than we'd bargained for.

Yes, I'd accepted Jesus on our wedding night, but I definitely didn't wake up perfect the day after. There were many hidden layers in my heart that had to be peeled away in order for me to see things from the right perspective. I still had an angry, self-serving attitude from things that had happened to me before I met Larry. I was a Christian, but I hadn't really developed a one-on-one relationship with the Lord. And I certainly didn't understand the vital spiritual principle, "But seek first His kingdom and His righteousness; and all these things shall be added to you" (Matt. 6:33).

I'll never forget a call I received from Larry's mother shortly after we were married. She said, "Barb, I'm praying for you. I pray that God will wrap His shield of protection around you and place His guardian angels beside you..." The whole time she was talking, I remember thinking, "Yeah, yeah, yeah...what have I gotten into?"

I wasn't ready for spiritual things, even though I was saved. Now, I understand and appreciate my mother-in-law. She's the sweetest, most godly woman I know. And I understand and respect Larry more than ever. I had to grow in faith to begin living according to godly principles—and these lessons weren't easy.

A case in point was the brand new Bible Larry gave to me four days before we were married. It was full size and had my name engraved on the cover—*I'd never received anything like this before.* On the inside, he wrote, "Barbara, God gave you to me and I am so happy. This is the greatest gift I could give you. This is the first time you'll see your new name in print. Love always, Larry." Then he closed by writing Philippians 1:3. When I looked it up (which, by the way, was the first time I can recall looking up a verse in the Bible!), it read, "I thank my God every time I remember you" (NIV). At the time, I thought it was a nice sentiment. Now, it means so much more.

I remember reading, "God gave you to me and I am so happy..." and cautiously thinking, "*Okay*..." I didn't get it. And I really didn't understand when he wrote, "This is the greatest gift I could give you..." I thought, "*Okay*...but I don't want a Bible. I want new clothes!" It scared me to see my name on the cover; I was threatened by it. Surely, my life was going to change. I thought I'd have to give up everything that had meant anything to me. Now I know the opposite is true. I had everything to gain—but I still had a long way to go. I didn't automatically embrace the Word of God in my life, and it definitely contributed to the issues we faced early in our marriage.

On the other hand, Larry had been burned so many times he didn't know how to trust me. That's when I began to reflect on what I believe are the two schools on trust: The first says, "I trust you until you give me a reason not to." The second says, "I don't trust you and you have to prove to me that you're trustworthy." I was from the first school and Larry was from the second. I couldn't understand why he didn't trust me! I certainly didn't think I'd given him any reason not to (and with my history in relationships, this was a big deal for me). Trust soon became our bone of contention.

Larry and I hadn't talked in detail about my past relationships, but he knew I liked partying and had dated numerous men. Maybe he remembered the time I took him to a company party (shortly after we began to date). I floated around the room like a social butterfly, hugging and talking to numerous men *and* women. I was trying to impress Larry with my popularity within my company, and literally left him standing in a corner of the room much of the evening. This angered and hurt him deeply, and caused our first fight. So thinking back, perhaps I set the stage for mistrust when we first married...but it wasn't intentional. I was just showing off, letting Larry know that he'd gotten a winner.

By our second year of marriage, during a trip to Jamaica, Larry threatened to leave me...right where we'd been walking on the beach! A man acknowledged me, and Larry figured I must have flirted with him first. I was devastated. I couldn't believe the man I'd fallen so deeply in love with didn't trust me! We had a terrible argument, and then I found myself standing on the beach wondering if Larry was going to leave me in Jamaica with no money or a way to get back to the States. It didn't matter, though. I remember thinking, "I'll find a way home and then divorce Larry afterwards."

Before meeting Larry, I used many of the men I dated just to get what I wanted. Some of them were good people, but I didn't care. I

> *Love endures long and is patient and kind...*
> 1 Cor. 13:4, Ampl.

> *True love restores, even when it has been wrongly accused...it endures all things.*

> *Things from our past had to die before we could experience new life in our marriage. And now I can say, it was worth every tear.*

> *...let us lay aside every weight, and the sin which doth so easily beset us, and let us run with patience the race that is set before us, looking unto Jesus the author and finisher of our faith; who for the joy that was set before him endured the cross, despising the shame, and is set down at the right hand of the throne of God...*
> Heb. 12:1–2, KJV

stepped on them to get what I desired for the moment. And to make a long story short, I carried this selfish, self-serving attitude into our marriage. Then when I was ready to give up, God was just getting started. He was only beginning to do a work inside of me...He was teaching me about true love.

Larry and I patched it up, but not without a lot of pain and suffering. Neither one of us wanted yet another relationship to end in failure...so we stuck it out. Thank God! Looking back, I realize that Larry simply needed reassurance of my love for him—but I was so angry and self-consumed, I couldn't give it. I had to deal with some of my own issues before I could reach out and make Larry feel more secure in our relationship. I know now that true love restores, even when it's been wrongly accused. True love endures all things.

Jesus endured great pain and suffering on the cross, yet He still died and rose again to give us new life. He was wrongfully accused, yet He never stopped loving us. He did what was necessary to restore us to God. That's true love. Sometimes we have to go through great pain to understand this. With Larry and me, things from our past had to die before we could experience new life in our marriage. And now I can say, it was worth every tear.

Building A New Life Together

Larry had once pastored one of the fastest growing churches in America, and he shared that at the peak of his ministry he'd started to think success was due to his own efforts. God let him know that He could take everything away as quickly as it had been given—and He did. Larry lost everything. Ultimately, he worked through it and forgave himself: but he stopped pursuing his calling. That's when I met him.

Then about three years into our marriage, I started seeing how desperately Larry wanted to be back in God's favor. He needed to fulfill the call of ministry on his life.

A pattern began to emerge every Sunday. We'd sleep late, and then get up and talk about what we were going to do that day over coffee—but Larry would be so sad. At first, I couldn't understand why. This had been normal Sunday morning behavior for me. What was wrong with him? I really felt like Larry loved me, but I could see unhappiness written all over his face. Then Sunday would pass and he'd be happy again on Monday morning.

Since I was pretty much a new believer, I was a bit over my head when it came to understanding what Larry was going through. And he found it difficult to understand me at times, because we were so different. As time progressed, though, God gave us grace to deal with our relationship issues and begin building a stronger marriage. We definitely grew closer to each other as we drew closer to Him.

As my relationship with God deepened, I began to see the "real me," a human being that could use a lot of work. I realized that I had been more concerned about outer appearances than what was going on inside of my heart. Knowing God was definitely much more than simply going to church every week. It was far more important than the color of my hair, or which outfit I was wearing (all the things I'd been preoccupied with in the past). I began to understand that even though people could see my external persona, only God could see inside of my heart—*and that's what counted most*.

Every relationship takes love, work, and commitment—and it started with my relationship to Him. By seeking God first, everything else started coming into place. And God promises if we'll take care of the little things, He'll be faithful over the big things...and I was beginning to learn this lesson well.

Therefore I say unto you, Take no thought for your life, what ye shall eat, or what ye shall drink; nor yet for your body, what ye shall put on. Is not the life more than meat, and the body than raiment?...But seek ye first the kingdom of God, and his righteousness; and all these things shall be added unto you.
Matt. 6:25–33, KJV

...The LORD does not look at the things man looks at. Man looks at the outward appearance, but the LORD looks at the heart.
1 Sam. 16:7, NIV

Reflections

1. We all have selfish moments. What are a few of yours? Write them down.

2. Have you ever experienced selfishness in love, perhaps in your relationship now? A past relationship? Were you eventually able to gain an understanding of your partner's perspective? Record a few thoughts.

3. What one thing makes you realize when you're having a *Me, Me, Me* moment? Do you immediately stop and make amends, or wait until later? Be honest with yourself. Write down the results you've experienced, in either case.

4. Do you think people can be completely altruistic—that is, totally unselfish? Why?

5. To experience true love, what do you believe needs to happen? Put your thoughts on paper.

Chapter 2

There's More To Follow

Growing in Love: The Struggle To Conceive

I once heard a story about a man who decided to give some money to a poor preacher, but he didn't want to give it all at one time. So he sent $5.00 with a note saying, "There's more to follow." A few weeks later, he sent another $5.00 with another note saying, "There's more to follow..." Again, a few weeks later, he sent another $5.00 along with the same note until the entire amount of money had been sent.

As I continued in my marriage and walk with the Lord, I learned how true this was. It's like God was saying to me, "I forgive you of your sins, but there's more to follow. I adopt you into My family, but there's more to follow. I'm educating you for heaven and for your life here on earth, but there's definitely more to follow." Every blessing from God comes with this message. He expects us to develop and grow; producing more from what He's given us.

Jesus said in John 15:1–5, "I am the true vine, and My Father is the vinedresser. Every branch in Me that does not bear fruit, He takes away; and every {branch} that bears fruit, He prunes it, that it may bear more fruit....Abide in Me, and I in you. As the branch cannot bear fruit of itself, unless it abides in the vine, so neither {can} you, unless you abide in Me. I am the vine, you are the branches; he who abides in Me, and I in him, he bears much fruit; for apart from Me you can do nothing."

God was dealing strongly with me in the early years of my marriage, because He wanted

...No eye has seen, no ear has heard, no mind has conceived what God has prepared for those who love him...
1 Cor. 2:9, NIV

me to have a spirit of faithfulness and obedience. And that kept taking me back to Matthew 6:33, "...seek first His kingdom and His righteousness; and all these things shall be added to you." Step by step, He peeled those hidden layers from my heart and replaced them with righteousness—*and it didn't feel good.* At times, it was a wearisome process, but I learned with each new day that God's will for me was in His Word. I began to realize: As I learned to draw near to Him, He'd help me change. And as I changed, the love He'd given to Larry and me would grow even deeper.

At first, Larry and I were like any other married couple. We had a lustful love. Everything was new, mysterious, and exciting. However, after the "newness" of our relationship was gone, I began to get bored and fed up with the day-to-day realities of marriage. As a young child, I'd learned to escape from whatever I didn't want to deal with—just do what was good for me. This wasn't acceptable to God. So He required me to stand on His Word and make the right choices, instead of leaving when everything wasn't going my way.

Early Lessons in Humility

Humility wasn't my strong suit. I was a mover and a shaker. I was used to making things happen and taking what I needed to get things done. God really had to work with me. The fact is, I felt terribly insecure. My life was changing dramatically, and I felt I was losing control fast. Subconsciously, I was struggling to maintain my independence, but God was in the process of making me one with my husband. And He works in mysterious ways.

About a month after we got married, Larry came across some old pictures of me with ex-boyfriends and other male co-workers at company events. He had a real problem with it, because at the time, I was still traveling all over the country for my job. As Larry looked through the pictures, he wondered how many of these men I'd dated and still knew—and he didn't like it. So one by one, he started throwing them away. That's when I walked in. We had a huge argument. I felt invaded..."How dare you get into my stuff and throw it away! You didn't ask my permission! This is *your* problem, not mine," I declared. "You get it fixed!"

I reacted and accused Larry, instead of trying to understand his point of view. Whether he was right or wrong, we were in it together. In God's eyes, we'd become one flesh. And when our own flesh is experiencing pain, how do we handle it? *As gently as possible.* I definitely wasn't gentle with Larry, because I was used to doing whatever was necessary to get my own way. I had a lot to learn about humility.

Don't misunderstand: I'm not saying that as a wife, I'm not entitled to express my opinion. I'm saying that as a Christian and a wife, I had to learn how to communicate in a more constructive way—and that would come only through love and humility. Once I learned how to understand and respect Larry, I could then help him to understand me. Then together, we could arrive at the best solution. No, it wasn't about *Me, Me, Me* anymore. God was confirming this every day.

Paul said in Philippians 2:1–5, "If therefore there is any encouragement in Christ, if there is any consolation of love, if there is any fellowship of the Spirit, if any affection and compassion, make my joy complete by being of the same mind, maintaining the same love, united in spirit, intent on one purpose. Do nothing from selfishness or empty conceit, but with humility of mind let each of you regard one another as more important than himself; do not {merely} look out for your own personal interests, but also for the interests of others. Have this attitude in yourselves which was also in Christ Jesus..."

I've often said that I don't believe anyone can be purely altruistic. I know in my life, it seemed there was always some self-benefit hidden deep beneath the surface. Yet God was expecting this from me in my marriage, I'm sure because Christ had willingly sacrificed His life for me. Therefore, to become great in the kingdom of God I had to become a servant— and it started with my husband. I had to learn to give love without expecting anything in return. *I couldn't do it without God's help.*

Truth be told, neither can you, nor any human being for that matter. We absolutely need God to keep us in check and make sure our motives are pure. The book of Matthew teaches that even those who give to charities can do it simply to receive a hidden benefit— whether it's public exposure, a tax break, or something else. "Be careful not to do your 'acts of righteousness' before men, to be seen by them. If you do, you will have no reward from your Father in heaven. So when you give to the needy, do not announce it with trumpets, as the hypocrites do in the synagogues and on the streets, to be honored by men. I tell you the truth, they have received their reward in full" (6:1–2, NIV).

Only God is able to judge whether we're serving ourselves, or others; and He convicts us when we're not doing good things for the right reasons. God loved us so much that He gave up His only Son (Jn. 3:16). This is why only He can help us to love one another.

First Corinthians 13:4–8 says, "Love endures long *and* is patient and kind; love never is envious *nor* boils over with jealousy, is not boastful *or* vainglorious, does not display itself haughtily. It is not conceited (arrogant and inflated with pride); it is not rude (unmannerly) *and* does not act unbecomingly. Love (God's love in us) does not insist on its own rights *or* its own way, *for* it is not self-seeking; it is not touchy *or* fretful *or* resentful; it takes no account of the evil done to it [it pays no attention to a suffered wrong]. It does not rejoice at injustice *and* unrighteousness, but rejoices when right *and* truth prevail. Love bears up under anything *and* everything that comes, is ever ready to believe the best of every person, its hopes are fadeless under all circumstances, and it endures everything [without weakening]. Love never fails..." (Ampl.).

The Dilemma of The Virtuous Woman

Along with writing that beautiful note on the inside cover of my Bible, Larry and I ended up having discussions of a "virtuous woman" and submission. I also remember something being said about a wife's duty and role. "An excellent wife, who can find? For her worth is far above jewels. The heart of her husband trusts in her, and he will have no lack of gain. She does him good and not evil all the days of her life....She looks well to the ways of her household, and does not eat the bread of idleness. Her children rise up and bless her; her husband {also,} and he praises her, {saying:} 'Many daughters have done nobly, but you excel them all' " (Prov. 31:10–12 and 27–29).

    At the time, I didn't receive it well from Larry. It was so foreign to me, like aliens had invaded my life...and I was fighting it tooth and nail. I'd worked hard for years trying to achieve my educational and career goals, only to discover everything I believed about being a woman had been wrong. As a result, our first two years of

Charm is deceitful and beauty is vain, {but} a woman who fears the LORD, she shall be praised.
Prov. 31:30

marriage were extremely difficult. We almost didn't make it. And to be honest, I struggled with this issue well beyond that. God was definitely dealing with me, breaking an old, unhealthy lifestyle and preparing me for what would come. This was a very painful process.

When the prophet Jeremiah received his call, God said to him, "See, I have appointed you this day over the nations and over the kingdoms, to pluck up and to break down, to destroy and to overthrow, to build and to plant" (1:10). This means when the Lord is doing something new in your life, He often tears down before He builds—that way you've got a great foundation. No one forced me to marry Larry or receive Jesus into my heart. I made these decisions, but I didn't initially see that God was leading me. He had a purpose for my life, and everything I experienced was bringing it to pass. The more I came to know the Lord, the clearer I heard His voice...and with each lesson, my trust and obedience continued to grow.

I gradually learned that I could do all things through Christ, who gives me strength (see Phil. 4:13). And I began to understand many wonderful things could follow in our marriage as I put God and Larry first in my life. I came to realize that if couples would simply look to the Word of God, there would be fewer failed marriages, less wayward children, and in general, a much better world. Jesus said, "...'If you abide in My word, you are My disciples indeed. And you shall know the truth, and the truth shall make you free' " (Jn. 8:31–32, NKJ).

I'm eternally grateful that Larry and I fought hard through the storms to keep our relationship intact. Now, we have such deep respect and admiration for each other. Love hasn't failed us yet!

Our First Efforts To Conceive

Larry expresses his generosity in many ways. When we were first married, he was forty-three and had two sons from his first marriage. He simply wanted to get on with his life, preferably without starting over again in terms of children. I, on the other hand, was nine years younger with no children from my first marriage. I desperately wanted to have a child of our own, so I wouldn't let the idea rest. There was one, major problem, though. Larry had had a vasectomy about fifteen years before we met.

I pleaded with Larry to find out if he was a candidate for vasectomy reversal, and he did. During his appointment, the doctors said that although it could be reversed, conception would be difficult because many years had passed since his initial procedure (which meant his motility rate would probably be significantly lower). Over and above this, they told him that reversal was much more complicated: Everything that had been disconnected in the original procedure had to be reconnected by microscopic surgery. I still laugh when I remember Larry saying, "Must they call it micro? Why not macro?"

Still, the doctors encouraged us to proceed. There were many risks, but Larry went through it for me. That's what I call true love.

After Larry's surgery and three weeks of agony, he recovered. Unfortunately, the results weren't at all what we'd expected. As time passed, Larry and I became frustrated and questioned their recommendations. Obviously, a person that's had a vasectomy three or five years prior to the reversal procedure would have experienced more success than we did.

We began looking into fertility treatments. That's when we learned that Larry's sperm count only had a five percent motility rate. This, in turn, meant we had a zero to slim chance of ever conceiving a child. Undaunted, I decided to focus on making my body more receptive and fertile. I had numerous exams that determined I shouldn't have any problem conceiving a child. To up my odds, I was given oral applications of a drug called Clomid. There were a few possible side effects: multiple egg fertilization (resulting in multiple births), and the more common things like slight weight gain and nausea—but all in all, it wasn't bad.

There were days I had to take my body temperature, or stay in bed, but I didn't want to make a big deal about it. I was very aware of what I needed to do, and I'd heard all the wives' tales...so I tried everything possible, including eating the right foods and exercising regularly—anything that would make my body more receptive to conception. Sometimes I felt like I was breaking apart inside, but I didn't want my emotions to create drama for Larry. I wanted him to know how much I loved him, and that I needed him for much more than making a baby.

Then in March 1998, while we were in the process of starting our church, the breakthrough came. I can't begin to explain how excited I was to see that little blue line emerge on my home pregnancy test! I kept re-checking it just to be sure, "Is that really a line?" I questioned myself. "Sure it is...but maybe it should be darker. I'll re-read the instruction sheet..." What a process! By the time Larry got home, I took it to him and asked, "Does this look like a dark blue line to you?" He looked at me with those romantic, blue eyes and said, "Honey, I believe you're pregnant." We held each other like we never had before.

Excited, I called everyone we knew, even before getting confirmation from my doctor. I couldn't contain myself. We were going to have a baby!

A Strange Turn of Events

Then one Wednesday (about three months into the pregnancy), something strange started happening. Larry and I had just returned from a vacation, so we were wrestling with whether or not we'd go to church that night. He was laying on the bed reading a book and I remember laying next to him and saying, "Larry, I don't feel right. I'm cramping a little bit, and this is unusual because I haven't cramped in so long." He told me to stay where I was and asked, "Do you think it's something to worry about?" I was afraid to answer. I laid still, but the cramping continued, so I decided to call the doctor.

I'd been monitoring the cramping, so I told him it started "light" and then became "a little more severe." He advised me to stay off of my feet; to actually put them up and rest...and I did. Yet somehow I knew something terrible was wrong. I hadn't cramped in weeks. I told Larry to go on to church without me.

About thirty minutes after he left, severe cramping took me into the bathroom. I was almost doubling over. I knew what was happening, especially when the bleeding began. So I just sat there and cried. How could this happen? Surely, God wasn't playing a joke on me...after all we'd done to conceive this baby! An eternity seemed to pass. Finally, I managed to get up before Larry got back home.

When he walked in the door, our eyes met. I was sitting on the couch, numb. Larry took three steps and fell to his knees in tears. He knew I'd lost the baby.

I made a doctor's appointment the next morning and went in for tests. It was confirmed...I wasn't pregnant anymore. I'd lost a lot of blood, but I still hadn't expelled the fetus. The doctor decided to let me expel it naturally, which meant I had to carry a bottle of formaldehyde at all times. I knew it was necessary, but it was almost too much to bear. Whenever a clot or anything unusual emerged, I was told that I should gather it up and preserve it in the bottle. That way, the doctor could test it and perhaps come up with a reason for my miscarriage as well as safeguards for future pregnancies.

After several days, the bleeding finally stopped, but I was never able to get a decent sample. I didn't really know what to expect, and that scared me. I remember thinking, "Am I going to see clots, or something that resembles a fetus?" The doctor had given me information, but this was new to me. I was so uncertain. It was my first pregnancy, and my first miscarriage. I could read, listen to stories, and get the best of advice—but I still had to experience it for myself. Doctors and nurses have seen thousands of miscarriages, but I had to live through it, not knowing exactly how my body would respond.

When I returned to the doctor for a follow-up appointment, they confirmed my body had cleaned itself out naturally. Everything was fine. Interestingly, I seemed to have known this all along, too. I had no trouble throwing the formaldehyde away, although it seemed to symbolize the end of something in my life. On one hand, I was almost relieved the incident was over. I could throw away that part of my life and start fresh. On the other hand, it felt like I was throwing away my hopes and dreams. It was bittersweet: a bad thing and a good thing—yet again, God helped me through it.

One of the hardest things was telling people I'd lost the baby...especially after announcing to everyone I could think of that I was pregnant. Larry and I were crushed, but somehow, God used this experience to strengthen us and bring us closer together.

Chapter 2 / There's More To Follow

A Glimpse of God's Blessings

Larry and I are both deer hunters. We know that when we're hunting, we may only get glimpses of a few deer, even though there are many in the woods. Some of God's blessings are like this. They're cleverly disguised. Sometimes you only get a glimpse of what He has for you, but if you stay in tune with Him, you'll consistently see His blessings all around you. And as you see His blessings, you'll always be thankful. When I think back on this experience, that's one of the most valuable lessons I learned.

James 1:2–4 reminds us, "Dear brothers, is your life full of difficulties and temptations? Then be happy, for when the way is rough, your patience has a chance to grow. So let it grow, and don't try to squirm out of your problems. For when your patience is finally in full bloom, then you will be ready for anything, strong in character, full and complete" (TLB).

Through it all, God perfected my faith. It wasn't easy, but I learned to trust that He had everything in control. "And we know that God causes all things to work together for good to those who love God, to those who are called according to {His} purpose" (Rom. 8:28). I took comfort in knowing that God always knows best. Maybe something in our little one wasn't developing properly, and God, in His incredible wisdom, carried our baby's soul back to heaven.

I didn't have much time with our little one on earth, but I know he or she is with God. And one day, we'll be reunited.

Philippians 4:6–7 encouraged me, "Do not fret *or* have any anxiety about anything, but in every circumstance *and* in everything, by prayer and petition (definite requests), with thanksgiving, continue to make your wants known to God. And God's peace [shall be

In everything give thanks: for this is the will of God in Christ Jesus concerning you.
1 Thess. 5:18, KJV

> *I know how to be abased and live humbly in straitened circumstances, and I know also how to enjoy plenty and live in abundance. I have learned in any and all circumstances the secret of facing every situation, whether well-fed or going hungry, having a sufficiency and enough to spare or going without and being in want. I have strength for all things in Christ Who empowers me [I am ready for anything and equal to anything through Him Who infuses inner strength into me; I am self-sufficient in Christ's sufficiency].*
> Phil. 4:12–13, Ampl.

yours, that tranquil state of a soul assured of its salvation through Christ, and so fearing nothing from God and being content with its earthly lot of whatever sort that is, that peace] which transcends all understanding shall garrison *and* mount guard over your hearts and minds in Christ Jesus" (Ampl.).

Larry and I continued to hope in God and try for another baby...and I learned to love my husband in ways I never thought were possible. I also learned that even in my darkest hour, God could give me incredible peace. Yes, our life had taken a few unexpected turns; but as I kept my eyes on Jesus, I was filled with hope for great days ahead! At every turn, I knew God would always be there.

Reflections

1. First Corinthians 2:9 says, "No eye has seen, no ear has heard, no mind has conceived what God has prepared for those who love him" (NIV). What does this scripture say to you?

2. We're a very "scratch my back, and I'll scratch yours" society. When was the last time you freely gave to someone (i.e., a spouse, friend, or relative) without expecting anything in return?

3. For some, conception is easy. For many, the struggle to conceive is a very painful process. Is there comfort in these situations? What do you believe it is?

4. Have you or someone you know suffered a miscarriage? What was the healing process?

Chapter 3

Oh Lukey Bob, Oh Lukey Bob

Enduring Love: Our Unexpected Miracle

Miracles can come in small packages...I know ours did, especially after trying for years to have a child of our own. (I guess it helped that I'm a strong, confident person who doesn't easily give up!) Actually, Larry and I tried for about nine more months after the miscarriage, and I was getting ready to look into adoption. At times, I thought, "What a cruel joke..." Larry and I couldn't have a baby at all, and then after almost five years of painstaking effort, we'd conceived and then lost the baby. At times, I wanted to ask God, "Why are You doing this?"—*then one day another blue line emerged.*

    The question was whether Larry and I would tell people that I was pregnant again. We were hesitant to share our good news at first, but then decided, "Why not?" I figured if I lost the baby this time, I'd need to have caring friends around me. *I'd need their prayers.* So we started sharing our exciting news. Satan wasn't going to steal my joy, not for one moment!

    I received an email once that kind of sums up the way we felt. "A baseball in my hands is worth about $6.00. A baseball in Mark McGuire's hands, about $16 million. A basketball in my hands is worth about $9.00. A basketball in Michael Jordan's hands, around $33 million. A golf club in my hands is just a club in my hands, while a golf club in Tiger Woods' hands is proof of four major championships. Nails in my hands are worth nothing, but nails in the hands of Christ brought salvation for an entire world! Guess it all depends on whose hands it's in." Larry and I weren't about to lose our peace—*we knew Whose hands we were in!*

An Unexpected Turn

I was careful to do everything to the best of my ability: I ate right, tried my best to get plenty of rest, and did everything the doctor advised me to do. Then as I was just entering my eighth month of pregnancy, my water broke. I had just taken a bath and was drying off when I felt water trickling down my legs. Thinking it was just the bath water, I finished up and went to eat dinner with Larry (he'd cooked dinner for me that night). Deep down, though, I knew something wasn't right. I was clearing the dinner plates from the table and...swoosh! A gush of water hit the floor.

"Why is this happening?" I wondered, as we scrambled to call the doctor. I still had eight weeks to go! The baby couldn't come now! All the way to the hospital, I kept wondering, "Is this it? What on earth is happening?" I was so scared...I just wanted the baby to be okay. Somehow, though, peace kept rising within me. I knew God would take care of the baby and that everything was going to be all right.

When we arrived at Trinity Medical Center, I got an education. They told us my experience wasn't all that abnormal. In fact, one of the books I read, *What To Expect When You're Expecting*, stated that early miscarriages are very common, "...occurring in as many as 40% of conceptions."[1] An early miscarriage can go unnoticed, passing for an unusually heavy or crampy menstrual cycle. Later miscarriages happen between the end of the first trimester and twenty weeks.

And the peace of God, which surpasses all comprehension, shall guard your hearts and your minds in Christ Jesus.
Phil. 4:7

Many other women have premature births. Although the book sites more babies are born late than early, the number of preterm births has increased over the years. It states, "One third of preterm births occur because labor begins early; one third because the membranes rupture prematurely; and one third because of a maternal or fetal problem."[2] Why this happens is relatively unknown, in spite of efforts aimed at preventing these types of births. You can, however, increase your odds of carrying a pregnancy to term by practicing proper nutrition, abstaining from substance abuse, and getting good prenatal care.

The general rule of thumb is when your water breaks, you should have the baby within 24 to 48 hours (due to the risk of infection). With me, however, the doctors were in no rush. I was admitted, settled into a room, and then hooked up to several different monitors to keep track of our vital signs. They told me everything appeared to be okay for the moment; they were just keeping a close eye on us. A sonogram the next day revealed that a small amount of water had begun to build back up, but not enough to sustain the baby. Still, he was doing great.

The doctors were amazed. And since our vital signs were good, we opted to wait longer and let Luke continue to develop. (With today's technology, a baby born at thirty-two weeks is risky, but still has a good chance of survival. A child born at thirty-four weeks has an even better chance—so we opted for the second.) If, however, something changed in our vitals, they were prepared to perform an emergency Caesarean section. In the meantime, I was the best incubator in the world for our little one...and he needed as much time as possible to continue developing. Every day in the womb made a tremendous difference.

I stayed in the hospital for what turned out to be two more weeks under strict orders of complete bed rest. I could only get up to use the restroom. Friends would visit and bring me things to do: magazines, cross-stitch, electronic golf, you name it, I got it. They even brought me chocolates and Wendy's shakes—and these helped, temporarily. Soon, I was exhausted. Nurses were checking me every two hours, even at night. Yet and still, I continued to pray, "Lord, let Luke stay in my tummy just one more day. He needs to grow."

Larry tried staying overnight with me, but his 6 foot 5 inch, 200+ pound body just wasn't built to sleep on the tiny, four-foot sofa bed. It was a disaster for his back—he just couldn't do it. We even tried to get another room, but none were available. So Larry visited me during the day and slept at home. I longed to be with him in our own bed. I was so lonely and scared; I cried every night. Still, I was thankful God was giving us more time for Luke to develop. Our baby was going to be okay.

Even happy times can bring sadness, worry, and stress; but once again, I was learning that I could get through anything with the strength of the Lord.

Those two weeks were only a blink of history, but I have to admit, sometimes it seemed like an eternity. Even happy times can bring sadness, worry, and stress; but once again, I was learning that I could get through anything with the strength of the Lord. Little by little, hidden layers in my heart were still being peeled away. And I took comfort in knowing that the Lord isn't early, and He's never late—He's always right on time.

Oh, Lukey Bob

At 5:00 in the morning on June 14, 1999, I began to feel early labor pangs. This was it! Luke Marlin Norrell was coming into the world. Yet I knew the drill, and didn't want to give birth on an empty stomach (imagine that!). Knowing the doctors would only allow me to eat cups of ice (once I revealed I was in labor), I waited until well after breakfast to break the news. At 7:00 a.m., I enjoyed bacon, eggs, pancakes, a muffin, coffee, and juice! Then I sipped my coffee until about 9:00 a.m. and made the happy announcement.

My body was progressing naturally in the labor process, but the doctors decided to induce me further by using a drug called petocin. They wanted to avoid any unnecessary distress to Luke's underweight, underdeveloped little body. Fifteen hours later, I was able to push him out into the world—with my mom on one leg and Larry on the other. I remember closing my eyes and pushing with everything that was in me. I wanted Larry to be so proud of me at that moment; he hadn't witnessed the births of his older sons, so this was an important time for us. I went into my own world, keeping my eyes closed and pushing with gusto...until I became aware of their voices saying, "Barb...you can open your eyes now. The baby's here!" Apparently, I'd kept pushing a couple minutes after Luke was born!

Lukey Bob was tiny, 5 pounds and 2 ounces to be exact, yet he was so beautiful. (Actually, they told me later he was a good size for a preemie.) I caught a glimpse of Luke as they held him in front of me briefly before whisking him away to the hospital's Neonatal Intensive Care Unit (NICU). I wouldn't hold him until the third day (for about five minutes), but Larry and I were overjoyed at Luke's arrival. For me, Lukey Bob is a true miracle—*the most perfect gift from God*, "But whatever is good and perfect comes to us from God, the Creator of all light, and he shines forever without change or shadow" (Jam. 1:17, TLB).

In case you're wondering, "What's with the name, Lukey Bob?" dad came up with it. Larry's

> *Lo, children are an heritage of the L*ORD*: and the fruit of the womb is his reward....Happy is the man that hath his quiver full of them: they shall not be ashamed, but they shall speak with the enemies in the gate.*
> Ps. 127:3–5, KJV

a good-ole boy from Arkansas and he envisioned Luke going to small 2A schools in rural areas (similar to the ones he'd attended as a boy), so that Luke would have a better opportunity to "be somebody" and become a star football player! When this happened, he'd definitely need a cool name! Larry could just imagine hearing the announcer at a Friday night game, "...and Lukey Bob throws! It's good! Lukey Bob has just nailed it for a touchdown to win the game!" (Honestly, when I first heard it, I couldn't imagine calling our son Lukey Bob...but now, I use it all the time!)

Two days after giving birth, I was released from the hospital...*without Luke*. It was so difficult to leave without him. When I got home, though, Larry had a wonderful surprise for me. He'd installed a big, whirlpool tub in our bathroom (among doing several other, thoughtful things). He wanted to make me comfortable, and it helped a lot. So one day not long after, I drew a bath and called my sister. When she answered, I started wailing, "I'm sitting in the most wonderful bathtub, I have the whirlpool turned on, and my husband has done so much to make my homecoming special...but I still don't have my baby!" I hated being without Luke.

For the next two weeks, I spent every day at the hospital, praying for Luke, holding him (eventually for up to 30 minutes at a time), and singing sweet lullabies. Over and over again, I apologized to Luke that he had to be in the hospital without me. I remember it was so awkward picking him up! I had to work around all those wires to avoid ripping them off his little body when lifting him out of the incubator. I had to be so careful. Afterwards, I'd go home, take care of a few things—look in the nursery at Luke's empty bassinet—and start crying again. I just wanted my baby to be at home with me!

> *Sometimes no matter how much God blesses us, we feel it's not enough. We want more.*

As the days edged on, I struggled with discouragement.

Sometimes no matter how much God blesses us, we feel it's not enough. We want more. God had been so faithful to us in so many ways! He blessed us with Luke, kept him safe in my womb for two weeks after my water had broken, and gave me a miraculous delivery. Yet I was miserable that I couldn't bring Luke home.

Every day I'd make myself look on the bright side. I could make it through, I just needed God to take one more step with me, just one more...and He did, every time. Throughout this process, I was pumping breast milk and taking bottles to the NICU. Finally, they had so much milk in their freezer, I was told to stop bringing bottles—but I still had to pump several times daily to keep my milk from drying up. I had so much milk in our freezer at home! One day, I just broke down. I couldn't take it any more.

Then I remembered the wonderful medical staff. Those doctors and nurses were a godsend! They took such excellent care of Luke (and other babies in the NICU) twenty-four hours a day. I prayed for them all the time. And when I was at the hospital, I built relationships with them. I knew all the shifts. Every time I'd go to the hospital, I'd be thinking, "What wonderful people!" God helped me through it, every step of the way, by gently reminding me of our many blessings. Finally, they told me I could bring Luke home. I couldn't believe it!

When I look back on this time, I think of Psalm 103: "Bless the LORD, O my soul: and all that is within me, *bless* his holy name. Bless the LORD, O my soul, and forget not all his benefits: who forgiveth all thine iniquities; who healeth all thy diseases; who redeemeth thy life from destruction; who crowneth thee with lovingkindness and tender mercies; who satisfieth thy mouth with good *things; so that* thy youth is renewed like the eagle's" (vs. 1–5, KJV). I learned, once again, to bless God in everything—because during that precious time, it took everything I had within me to bless Him. I'm still thanking God for His tender mercies.

Luke's Homecoming

It was June 28, two weeks after his birth, and I was rushing to Target to buy a car seat in order to bring Luke home that day. I was so excited and in such a hurry that I tripped in the parking lot and ended up sprawled out on the pavement. A guy asked me if I was okay, but all I could think about was Luke. I just wanted to bring our baby home! I didn't even know what to do with the car seat once I bought it—didn't know how to use the straps...nothing! I didn't worry about it, though. When I got to the hospital, I knew one of the nurses would show me how to get tiny Luke into this crazy contraption.

A few hours later, we were in the front seat of our 1994 Ford Ranger Pickup making our way home—me, Luke (in his car seat), and the apnea monitor. There were no air bags, but we were safe. Luke and I were sitting high above the world. The thirty-minute drive from Plano to Lucas would be a piece of cake, *I thought*—until the apnea monitor started going off.

An apnea monitor is normal procedure for preemies; it sounds a loud beep whenever the baby stops breathing. I'd been trained on how to use the monitor at the hospital, along with cardio pulmonary resuscitation (CPR). This was good preparation for a new mom, but it didn't quite address the emotional element. My hormonal changes were still in full swing, and that definitely didn't help on our way home.

Lukey Bob's apnea monitor went off five times before we got to the house. A thirty-

The thirty-minute drive from Plano to Lucas would be a piece of cake, I thought—until the apnea monitor started going off.

Chapter 3 / Oh Lukey Bob, Oh Lukey Bob

minute trip turned into three, hair raising hours! Every time the monitor went off, I'd pull off the road and shake him. That was the drill (I'd been told shaking restarted the breathing). Preemies aren't fully developed, so they can literally forget to breathe...and when that happens, you have to be ready. So pulling off the road during these moments of terror was more than a good idea! By the time we got home, I was a mess. I got Luke in the house and then just sat and stared at him. "Now what do I do?" I wondered. I'd prayed so hard for God to give me a baby! Now we were at home, and I was clueless. I broke down in tears...again.

Barbara Johnson, one of my favorite Christian authors, had a chapter in one of her books entitled, *Who Are These Kids, and Why Are They Calling Me Mom?* I laugh when I think of this now, because it's crossed my mind so many times. As I watch our healthy, energetic three year old tearing up his room (or pouring water all over the bathroom), I think to myself, "Who is this kid? And why is he calling me Mom?"

In the beginning, though, I was definitely walking on eggshells. Luke stayed on the apnea monitor for two months. By that time, I'd become very familiar with CPR and had taught Larry, his mother, my mother (and whoever else needed to know), how to care for Luke. We'd alerted the telephone and electric companies, fire department, and emergency medical personnel about Luke in the event of a power outage. We were a priority on everybody's list. It was touch and go for a while. Little Luke just couldn't be handled like the average baby.

I couldn't just pick him up, so bathing and dressing were major projects. Every time I handled him or changed his clothes, I had to work around cathodes, putting new tape on the monitor wires as needed. The wires were color-

It was touch and go for a while. Little Luke just couldn't be handled like the average baby.

51

coded: there was a little yellow one, and a little red one—both with coordinating tapes to be attached to specific areas on Lukey's chest. They monitored his heartbeat and breathing. I had to work around these wires all the time. Sometimes I felt detached from my son, because I could never be in close contact with him—not until we came through those first couple of months. I couldn't just embrace Luke; I always had to think of his safety first. It was a challenge, to say the least.

Added to this, since I hadn't been able to feed him directly from my breast in the hospital, Luke had grown accustomed to drinking my milk from a bottle. Actually, he had been fed from a tube for a while immediately after birth, and then he went to the bottle. When I brought him home, I had to transition him from the bottle to the breast, and it wasn't easy. Luke didn't like it one bit. He wanted the bottles back. I didn't want to produce milk, only to pump and bottle feed him. I was determined Luke and I could work through it.

One morning, I remember watching a story about the famous bicyclist, Lance Armstrong, beating cancer and winning the Tour de France. As he was giving his victory speech, I thought, "This man has overcome cancer and won the Tour de France, and I'm sitting here griping about not being able to get my baby to breast feed. Let's put this all into perspective, Barb.." I decided right then and there that nothing was going to stop me. Luke was either going to breast feed, or go without. We were going to get on the other side of this mountain!

We worked and worked at it, through Luke's stubbornness, my breast infections...whatever stood in the way of victory! I remember getting three baseball size lumps in my breasts. I refused to quit. I remember calling 800 numbers at 3:00 a.m., crying, "I'm having the worst time breast feeding!" They kept encouraging me, "Keep doing it," they'd say—because even with an infection, it's possible to keep breast-feeding. I tried cabbage leaves, warm shower massages...you name it—and ultimately it all paid off. Luke and I finally broke the barrier and he stayed on total breast milk for ten months! It was such an accomplishment...and it brought us closer together.

    I really enjoyed breastfeeding. It was so convenient! I'd be driving down the highway with Luke and when he was hungry, I could just pull over, lift that handy T-shirt, and take care of him. I could be talking on the phone and feeding Luke at the same time. It got to the point that I took Luke everywhere with me—I even breast fed him behind clothes racks when I went shopping! I remember thinking, "Breastfeeding is the greatest thing since sliced bread!" Bye-bye pumps, hello freedom.

    What a joy motherhood can be! Still, I've never had a harder position, especially since I didn't have Luke until I was 39. Now, I'm over forty with a toddler. Daily nap times are "Praise Jesus" moments for me! Yet I'm eternally grateful for Luke. By God's grace, Lukey Bob is absolutely healthy and beautiful. I thank God for every day he's in my care.

    Larry and I have a song we made up for Luke, and I want to share it with you. It goes with the melody of, "Oh Tynenbaum, Oh Tynenbaum." Here it is:

> *Oh Lukey Bob, Oh Lukey Bob*
> *You are our favorite child.*
> *Oh Lukey Bob, Oh Lukey Bob*
> *We sure do love your smile.*
> *We love you when you're near to us,*

Because of that, we give you our bus,
Oh Lukey Bob, Oh Lukey Bob
You are our favorite child.

Actually, we have three sons (including Larry's sons, Larry Glenn and Bobby). So when we sing this song, we fill in a different name as needed (no favoritism here!). Larry Glenn is twenty-five, Bobby is twenty-two, and you know Luke...he's the one that's still tearing up our kitchen! All three of them have been bequeathed our huge, Silver Eagle, customized passenger bus (Larry tore out all 40 seats and renovated the inside for our future traveling pleasure). I guess they'll have to work out the details of sharing later! We're sure they'll be more than happy to do it.

Getting To Know You...Better

Lukey Bob's arrival took Larry's and my relationship to a new level. We loved each other deeply, as well as our new son, but we still had to endure "growing pains." On top of the emotional and physical changes of motherhood, I was so unsure about everything I was doing. It was all new to me. Again, God continued to expose new layers of my heart that I needed to submit to Him. Would this process ever end?

Remembering that Larry hadn't initially wanted to start over with a family, I put extra pressure on myself to do everything that was needed for Luke. I didn't want Larry's life to be interrupted any more than was absolutely necessary. I wanted everything to be smooth sailing for him so that he'd feel we made the right decision. So I tried to be the perfect mother, immediately meeting every need, so that Larry wouldn't even know Luke and I were there. I lost a lot of sleep, and ultimately it affected our relationship—but it was all self-imposed. Larry never required this of me.

The good thing is Larry and I are great communicators. So after we came through the first, trying months, we started communicating more about our needs as new parents. If we hadn't been intimate in a while, we'd sit down and talk about it. And then we'd work out a plan to spend some time together. I just love that about Larry. We still do this now. I can easily call him on any given day and say, "We haven't made love in two weeks. We need to be together," or vice versa.

Larry and I have learned how to be successful parents, partners, and lovers. Each is vitally important. And each helps to keep things exciting and appealing in our relationship. I don't ever want to get so comfortable around Larry that I don't care about my appearance, or stop treating him like the loving, desirable man that he is. No matter what, couples should always work to maintain this. It's well worth it.

Finally, with Lukey Bob well and routines coming into place, everything seemed to be settling down. I started learning how to enjoy the moment. Looking back, I think that's one of the things God was trying to teach me during this process. In "seeking first" His kingdom, it's all about the journey. And as we put God first, He faithfully gave us what we needed every step of the way.

When I think of the love I have for Luke, I'm overwhelmed to tears. This kind of love endures all things, no question about it. I'd easily give my life for my child...just like Jesus gave His life for us. *Can we ever imagine the depths of His love?*

Who shall separate us from the love of Christ? Shall tribulation, or distress, or persecution, or famine, or nakedness, or peril, or sword?....Nay, in all these things we are more than conquerors through him that loved us. For I am persuaded, that neither death, nor life, nor angels, nor principalities, nor powers, nor things present, nor things to come, nor height, nor depth, nor any other creature, shall be able to separate us from the love of God, which is in Christ Jesus our Lord.
Rom. 8:35–39, KJV

---

[1] Eisenberg, Arlene, Murkoff, Heidi E., and Hathaway, Sandee E. *What To Expect When You're Expecting*, p. 347. Workman Publishing Company, Inc., New York, NY. Copyright © 1984, 1988, 1991, 1996.
[2] Eisenberg, Murkoff, and Hathaway, p. 218.

Reflections

1. Do you believe in miracles? Write a few reasons why.

2. Are you able to readily see God's blessings at work in your life? Have you been blessed, or are you still waiting for a blessing? Record your thoughts.

3. Think about the last time you went through a trying situation. What were some of the emotions you felt? How did you get through it?

4. Do you feel like the "storms" in life make you a stronger person? Bring you closer to God? Why?

Chapter 4

Can't You Understand, I Want To Be A Mom?

Labors of Love: Discovering What Matters Most

Yes, some of life's richest blessings are cleverly disguised—like motherhood, for example. I'd tell anybody, hands down; marrying Larry was one of the best things I've ever done in my life. And I can't begin to describe the depths of love and blessing Luke has given to me. Yet one day at a birthday party, something happened that turned my world upside down—and more hidden layers were brought to the surface.

A friend approached me and innocently asked what I'd been doing lately. To my surprise, I was stumped. I struggled with my answer for a few seconds, and then started telling her only about the things I thought would make me look "successful." I didn't tell her anything about being a new mother. The truth was, I didn't think being a stay-at-home mom was that much of an accomplishment. After all, I'd done many, important things in the business world. How could motherhood compare to that? *I didn't realize how wrong my thinking had been until that day.* If I could, I'd love to go back and change my response to: "I'm a mom, and proud of it!"

Without realizing it, I had drawn my whole identity from my career. I'd spent six, successful years at Southwest Airlines. Then shortly after marrying Larry, I left Southwest and began to learn the family roofing business. A

> *A friend approached me and innocently asked what I'd been doing lately....I didn't tell her anything about being a new mother....Without realizing it, I had drawn my whole identity from my career.*

57

year after that, I founded my own residential roofing company and expanded it to a thriving business by the year 2000. I had Lukey Bob in 1999—which made me start reevaluating my priorities. So I sold my business to stay at home and take care of my family...but a residue of the past still lingered in my subconscious mind. When my friend asked that question, the issue came to the surface.

I wanted to be a mother with everything that was in me! I just didn't realize my emotions needed time to catch up with my new lifestyle. Once again, I had to take a journey back to Matthew 6:33 and "seeking first" the priorities of God for my life. Layers started peeling away.

I wanted to be a mother with everything that was in me! I just didn't realize my emotions needed time to catch up with my new lifestyle.

Revisiting The Past...Again

In my early twenties and thirties, priority number one was looking out for myself. And it almost had to be that way, because I was on my own with no one else to take care of me. I didn't *know* God, and my family had fallen way down on my list of priorities. I remember my dad calling and reminding me, "You haven't been home, and we haven't seen or talked to you..." My work had become my top priority, because it brought money, and that's what I needed to survive. Unfortunately, this mindset had stayed with me, even after I'd married a wonderful man and given birth to Luke.

Honestly, though, my career had been another bone of contention since the beginning of our marriage. I was doing well at Southwest, traveling in a high profile position. I'd worked hard to build a professional image for myself. I wanted people to be attracted to me, see that I was doing a good job; but my priorities were all mixed up. Then Larry and I married, and the issue quickly came to a head. He was used to having someone by his side at home and in the ministry. On the other hand, I felt he was making it hard on me. Larry honestly couldn't understand why my job was so important. To make a long story short, we were married on December 29, 1994, and I made the decision to resign from Southwest on March 22, 1995.

It was traumatic for me, but I didn't realize how much so until years later at the birthday party. Actually, I think I had resentment for the first couple of years of our marriage. My major concerns were *me, myself, and I*—my priorities, my goals, and my career. In my mind, pursuing a successful occupation was still very much a part of me. After all, I'd worked since I was fifteen years old. Then almost overnight, at thirty-four years of age, I became a Christian and a devoted wife. To be honest, quitting my job literally blew me out of the water—because it intensified my struggle with identity and self worth.

After I left Southwest, I felt like a no good bum. A loser. I remember thinking, "What do I do now? Sit around the house all day?" I actually thought I'd made two critical mistakes—quitting my job *and* getting married. At times, I found myself wondering if Southwest would take me back! Interestingly, in doing this, I was canceling out everything I'd been traveling around the country, teaching other people to do. I needed to take my own advice: get a grip on my values and priorities, and manage my time and resources accordingly. Larry was such a wonderful husband, but sadly, he wasn't a priority in my life—so it was time for me to change.

Then a few years later, God blessed us with Luke. Still, I hadn't let go of the past. The fact is, I'd taken some pretty big risks for love. I was young in the Lord and scared of what might become of my life. God was gracious and helped me, one milestone at a time, so that I

> The fact is, I'd taken some pretty big risks for love. I was young in the Lord and scared of what might become of my life.

could bear it. This reminds me of what Jesus said to His disciples in John 16:12–13, "I have yet many things to say to you, but you cannot bear them now. When the Spirit of truth comes, he will guide you into all the truth; for he will not speak on his own authority, but whatever he hears he will speak, and he will declare to you the things that are to come" (RSV).

Shortly after I left Southwest, I went to work with Larry every day to learn his roofing business. I felt I needed to be out there working and bringing money into the family. This was the way I could contribute and justify quitting my career. I wasn't thinking about the importance of being a wife; *a completer.* So I continued working with Larry for a couple of years, and then established my own roofing company while we were trying to start a family. After my miscarriage, staying busy actually helped me. It took my mind off of things.

At the same time, however, my desire to have a child was becoming more focused than ever. That's when I realized I was off the hook—*I had an excuse for not working!* People could ask me if I worked, and I could simply say, "Oh no, we're trying to have a baby!" That seemed to make everything okay, so I started adding employees and gradually pulled away from the business.

Another reality check came in 1998 when I was asked to become the President of the Golf Association (at a country club where Larry and I were members). We had joined simply because we loved to play golf...but I took the position anyway. Looking back on my year as President, I had the right intentions, but didn't make any real changes. Nothing really happened, good or bad. I remember playing golf with the girls one day and thinking to myself, "Did I make a change here? Why did I become President? Did I have any influence on anything?" I'd had meetings all the time, but in the end, nothing really happened. Just the thought of being President and in charge was appealing. Although the position took me back to a leadership status, the Golf Association was no better because of me.

So after all had been said and done, I found myself at a birthday party stumbling for words at the simple question, "What are you doing now?" It stunned me to reality: My self worth had been wrapped up in "what I did" instead of who I was! This was a huge milestone...*and I knew God was still working on my heart.*

He'd been so faithful since I married Larry, but deep down, I really felt as if I'd been stripped of everything. My parents saw so much change in me they literally thought Larry had done some brainwashing! I definitely wasn't the "Barb" they used to know—which was actually a tremendous blessing! My emotions just needed to embrace the truth of who I was becoming in Christ...a blessed, *virtuous* woman.

If she asked the same question today, I'd declare that the greatest, most rewarding and fulfilling thing I've ever done is to be a mother. Every moment I spend with Luke is priceless, and every small thing I do for him is monumentally important: whether it's taking him to the park, cleaning up a wet spot on the floor, or picking up a mess in his playroom. Time spent with Luke is never in vain. My influence on him is extraordinary. Talk about a position of leadership! I'm making deposits that will last throughout eternity.

I once saw on the Biography Channel that Elvis Presley (i.e., the king of Rock and Roll) always remembered when his mother held his hand and walked with him to church or school. All that glamour, and Elvis remembered the simple things that impacted him most. *Mothers*

If she asked that same question today, I'd declare that the greatest, most rewarding and fulfilling thing I've ever done is to be a mother.

are vitally important, and motherhood is a wonderful gift. Sure, I get a little stir crazy at times, but then I stop and remind myself...this is a short, precious season of our lives. And if I miss these moments, I'll never get them back.

Getting Back To The Joy of The Moment

When I got pregnant with Luke, Larry tried to tell me, "Barb, with the baby, everything will change." I wasn't buying it. "Oh Larry, nothing will change," I quirked. I was a real go-getter and into physical fitness. So I continued, "I'll just strap that baby on my back and go rock climbing." Larry shot a look at me and said, "Okay." *I was so naïve!* I think many new moms are like this, thinking, "A baby won't change my life. It will have to adhere to my life, not vice versa." *The fact of the matter is your life changes every day you're a mother.*

Raising a child is hard. I remember taking Luke to a shoe store, thinking, "He wore a size 7 about a month ago; a 7-1/2 will do, he just needs something a little bit bigger." The clerk said, "Oh honey, that's too small..." She put a size 8-1/2 on him and said, "See, that fits great!" I was stunned. "What an awful mother I am!" I scolded myself, "I've had his size 8-1/2 foot in a size 7 shoe!" I really beat myself up for that.

One of my sisters seems to be the perfect mom; she always has everything in order. So one day I called her and said, "Isn't motherhood hard?" She replied, "No, not at all." Now I don't know if she was living in denial, or if she's truly this super-organized person that has it all together. For me, an older mother, it's been difficult. I'm always asking myself things like, "Is my son warm enough? Is the house temperature set at the right level? Does Luke have enough blankets at night?" My days are filled with questions, answers, and discoveries.

And then there are the toys...I used to totally stress myself out about them. Luke could care less. He can make a toy out of anything! He just loves the little button that opens the garage door. If I let him play with that button all day, I wouldn't have to bring one toy in the house! Children are such a wonder. The simplest things make them happy. I once heard about a survey where boys and girls were asked, "What's the number one gift that you would want from your parents?" Their top response was they wanted "more time." A toy is wonderful, but our time is by far the most excellent gift we can give to our children.

It's so easy to get caught up in the cares and obligations of life and lose the joy of the moment. When my friend asked me about what I was doing, that's exactly where I was—*caught up.* I'd lost the identity of my professional life, and felt unimportant. Instead of going to high-powered meetings, I was watching children's programs and going to McDonald's playgroups and birthday parties. And I was wondering, "What's it all about, anyway?"

Coming To Terms with What Matters Most

Don't ask what made me check for a lump. I wasn't good at doing self-breast exams (I did, however, have a mammogram at age 38 because I was considering getting breast implants—which I never got.) It was a Friday night in November 2001. More than a year had passed since Lukey Bob and I had made it through the breast-feeding challenge. As I checked my left breast, I was stunned to find a marble size lump on the upper, left side. Immediately, I thought maybe the breast

I once heard about a survey where children were asked "What's the number one gift that you would want from your parents?" Their top response was "more time."

It's so easy to get caught up in the cares and obligations of life and lose the joy of the moment.

Don't ask what made me check for a lump. I wasn't good at doing self-breast exams.

> *After all I went through to have a baby, was I now going to have to leave him behind in the care of his father?*

infections had caused something to form, or perhaps hormonal changes had caused a lump to appear.

The shock of the moment startled me. "Was this going to become the real test of my faith? Would I be diagnosed with breast cancer? After all those years partying, drinking, and smoking cigarettes, was I now about to pay the price? After all I went through to have a baby, was I now going to have to leave him behind in the care of his father?" These were extreme questions; nevertheless, they were darting through my mind like wildfire. And since it was Friday, I had to worry about it all weekend.

I called my doctor's office immediately on Monday, but was told he couldn't see me for a week. Frustration set in. I'd been with this same doctor for thirteen years, "Didn't they understand this was serious? Why couldn't he fit me in?" I marveled. I scrambled for the phone book and began searching for a doctor, any doctor. Then I called a friend and she gave me the name of a very good breast surgeon in Dallas—I called and got an answering machine. By then it was 10:00 a.m. And I was beginning to feel as if I'd wasted two hours of valuable time. "Doesn't anybody care about this lump?" I wondered.

Then I began to put everything in perspective. I thought, "My goodness, Barbara, you act like you're the only one who has ever found a lump. There are people all over the world that are dealing with this disease the best way they know how, and you're sitting here acting like this." It helped me, but I still knew it was serious, and that early detection would be critical. If breast cancer is caught early enough, the survival rate is good. I picked up the phone book again and kept searching.

Finally, Larry called and said his doctor could see me that afternoon...*thank God!* But before I shut the phone book, my eyes caught the name of a doctor that sounded strangely familiar. Where did I know that name? Then it hit me. This was the doctor who had delivered Luke! (Luke had arrived two weeks early, and my primary doctor was in the Philippines.) I felt this was one of those "glimpses" of God's blessings...so I called his office and said, "You're not going to remember me, but you stood in for Dr. So-and-so and delivered my baby two years ago, and I've found a lump..." "We'll be glad to see you in thirty minutes." Those were the words I'd been waiting for. God had made sure I saw his name before closing that book. This was totally a God thing!

    I drove to Trinity Medical Center, where I'd given birth to Luke, and rushed into the doctor's office. Waiting for him to see me, I glanced up at a diagram on the wall that showed what happens to a woman's body during pregnancy. I thought, "Well here I am again, but for an entirely different reason." I kept remembering the words of some close friends reassuring me, "Oh, we've had those. It's probably cystic." I wanted to ask the nurse, "Do you have a poster that shows what a woman's breasts look like with cancer?" I needed some answers. I needed reassurance that everything was going to be okay.

    I didn't get it. The doctor examined me and his first words were, "It doesn't feel cystic." Oh, my God! I thought surely he'd say it was a cyst. As he continued his examination he said, "...but it's moving, which is good, because cancer sticks to stuff. Normally, cancer doesn't move like this is moving." He recommended a mammogram, and told me it would probably take about a week to get an appointment. "I don't think I can wait a week," I piped in, "I'd worry too much...is there any way you could help get me in to see them?" He excused himself, and within five minutes, came back and said, "You can go downstairs right now."

Interestingly, instead of being relieved, I became more alarmed because they were able to see me more quickly than I thought. Within twenty minutes, I was downstairs filling out the paperwork. Then the hard part came...another wait. My mind was going haywire, "If it's not cystic, what could it be? I'll check myself right here in the waiting room...yeah, it's moving, so maybe it's not cancer..."

I started analyzing everybody that walked in the room, thinking, "What's her story?" I actually started a conversation with a young woman who was there with her mother. I asked, "Is everything okay?" She replied, "Oh yes. She had breast cancer two years ago and had a double mastectomy...we've been cancer free for two years." I was scared to death! I hadn't had any problems with my breasts until I was trying to breastfeed Luke—and that was just normal stuff.

What seemed to be an hour later, they called my name. I was led down a little, sterile, cold hallway to a tiny examination room. It had gray walls and floors, and was filled with machinery. "Why didn't they make this a little homier?" I pondered. It reminded me of McDonald's. I'd heard people say fast food restaurants are always painted in orange and yellow, because these colors make you not want to stay long. That way, you're in and out. Does that mean if they painted it blue, people would then want to hang out? Maybe dance for a while? I couldn't take it! This room was so cold; pretty much a normal examination room, but without the warmth of pictures, magazines, and a mobile hanging from the ceiling (like in most physician's offices).

My first thought was, "Okay, they're just examining you, telling you that you have cancer, and then you're out of here and on to the next phase." It was so impersonal. As I sat on that cold bed with tissue paper stretched over it, I was relieved when a young woman came through the door who was very friendly, warm, and caring. She began doing my mammogram. Overall, I spent at least two hours having my breasts (both of them) squeezed, pressed, pulled, stretched, pinched, and flattened. And since I'm so small breasted, I was truly amazed at how many ways they could do this! If I was full breasted, I could have just stood in front of that machine...but no, not me! I had to stick my whole rib up there, and then turn my neck, to get as close as possible.

Somehow, that hit a funny bone. I thought, "Well, this is humor...*I need humor.*" Humor was helping. The technician finished her series of pictures and then left the room to review them. As I waited, my mind started churning again about how stupid this place looked and how much I wanted to get out of it. "How could they have you wait in such a cold, gloomy room only to come back with the news that you have breast cancer?" I pondered. And then I started thinking of all the women who've ever been diagnosed with cancer: they were young, old, beautiful, homely, senators, housewives, and the like. "This breast cancer thing doesn't discriminate," I observed, "So why not me? I'm not special enough to avoid getting cancer...but did all of these women have to wait to hear their results in a room like this one?"

It was awful to think how many women had probably waited in a cold, gray atmosphere, only to be told they had a life threatening disease. I couldn't help thinking, "If a person's going to get the news she has breast cancer, she ought to be getting it in a five star hotel while being served a steak dinner! She needs to be treated right!" *That was it*—definitely a better way to handle it. If a woman had cancer, she'd be given a glass of red wine as soon as she walked into the office and invited to their luxurious resort for a special weekend retreat...*that* would lessen the impact of the fateful news. My mind was reeling! I thank God for bearing with me.

Still, I just couldn't imagine any woman having to sit there and hear a terrible report in a room like that. Maybe one day some aspiring business would explore a new angle on the "birthing room" concept, and create "cancer rooms" that are more patient-friendly. Something needed to change, because waiting in that room was definitely one of the scariest experiences of my life.

Then it came to me, "Gosh, how many women—especially the ones I just saw in the waiting room—have been sitting here doing the same thing, but don't have the Lord in their lives?" At this point, I realized Jesus was my only source of comfort. I started to hear Jeremiah 29:11, "For I know the plans I have for you," declares the LORD, "plans to prosper you and not to harm you, plans to give you hope and a future" (NIV).

Such a sense of peace came over me. I repeated this verse over and over, thinking, "God, You're not going to harm me because You have plans for me. There is hope for my future, so You're not harming me. Whatever I find out, it won't harm me. I will go through it with Your strength." I felt an incredible surge of confidence and security as I repeated this verse over and over again.

Then my emotions would try to kick back in. Even still, how would I react to the news? Would I go into shock? Would I cry? Would I need to look the part somehow in my reaction? Would I be totally calm, or go totally ballistic? And then I remembered another verse, "...I will

For I know the plans I have for you, declares the LORD, plans to prosper you and not to harm you, plans to give you hope and a future.
Jer. 29:11, NIV

never leave you nor forsake you," and the peace of the Lord came over me again (see Josh. 1:5, NIV).

The technician returned and said she needed to get more pictures. She took a few more, and as she was walking out the door, I asked, "Will I know something today?" "Yes." That was good, at least I'd know something right away. I started reciting Jeremiah 29:11 again, and then I remembered a feature I'd read about Peggy Fleming's bout with breast cancer in an issue of *People Magazine*. On the cover, there were pictures of several famous women and it read, "Surviving Breast Cancer." So many had survived it! *I wasn't alone.* Still, these women had to have been scared to death, sitting in cold rooms like the one I was sitting in—going through what I was experiencing at that very moment.

The technician returned, "Okay, the radiologist is going to come in and talk to you." The outcome wasn't as grim as I'd expected. He came in, did a sonogram, and during the procedure pointed out, "Do you see this little cluster of grapes? That's the marble lump that's formed...it's a cluster of cysts..." I was curious, "But the doctor said it didn't feel like cysts." He said, "Well there it is...and they're all hollow, so we don't have to extract liquid from them or anything. They're probably due to caffeine." Then he said at that point, they were nonmalignant, "Just watch your caffeine usage and the lump will probably dissolve."

I wanted to shout, "Praise Jesus!" at the top of my lungs, but I didn't want to freak anybody out. Inside I was singing, "Praise Jesus, praise Jesus, praise Jesus...Thank You, Lord, I'll never drink another diet soda in my life! I'll drink caffeine free everything." I asked the radiologist to re-check everything, thanked them, and left. When I got to the parking lot, I couldn't hold it in any longer—"Praise Jesus!" Then I got on my cell phone and began calling everyone, starting with Larry (who was on a one day business trip to Little Rock, Arkansas). When he heard the news, the phone went silent. Then he said, "I prayed all morning long..." (Larry worries deeply and he hurts when he thinks I'm hurting.) "Barb," he continued, "I would want this to be me rather than you or Luke. I just prayed that whatever happens would happen to me first, because I could handle that better than if anything happened to you or Luke."

We had a special celebration that evening. We put Luke to bed a little early and just spent time together. It was wonderful.

Four months later, I returned for a follow up mammogram and the lump hadn't changed. They told me to just keep checking it, because it could take a while to go down (a year or two, maybe, no one's certain). In the meantime, we've continued to monitor it at regular checkups. And I'm living life to the fullest!

Before having Luke and the breast cancer scare, I felt invincible. I'd always enjoyed great health (except for one experience when I had my tonsils taken out as a child). It just seemed so unlikely anything like this could ever happen to me. I excluded myself from cancer and major illnesses. Now I have a new outlook. I appreciate the little things more on a daily basis. I stop and smell the roses whenever I can.

I was like so many moms, rushing down the freeway, putting on makeup, yelling at my child in the back seat...all with the radio on. And then when the cell phone rang, I answered it without blinking an eye! We try to do everything at once, nearly missing dangerous collisions along the way. *Stop the car!* Pull over, put the makeup bag back in your purse, turn off the radio and cell phone, *and pull your child into your arms.* Then Praise God for bringing you out of a blind spot. That's what I did.

I'm glad I finally came to terms with what matters most. *I love being a mom!* Now I understand the joy that fills each moment I'm blessed to be with my family. Even difficult moments with Luke give me a sense of joy, because I know he's simply exploring his world. He's not trying to make me mad, or make my day awful. Luke's new at life. He'll get it one day. So when Luke is feeling good, I enjoy the moment. And when he's whiny, I respond to him the same way as if he were making me happy.

There's nothing better I can do in this world than shape the life of my child. Luke is a gift to my life; what I give to him will be *our gift* to the world. What could be more important than that?

I'm glad I finally came to terms with what matters most. I love being a mom!

Behold, children are a gift of the LORD; the fruit of the womb is a reward. Like arrows in the hand of a warrior, so are the children of one's youth.
Ps. 127:3–4

Her children rise up and bless her; her husband {also,} and he praises her, {saying:} Many daughters have done nobly, but you excel them all.
Prov. 31:28–29

Reflections

1. In what ways do you establish your identity, or self worth?

2. How do you define success?

3. What do you believe a woman's role is in life?

4. What matters most to you right now, in this season of your life?

5. If you've ever had a health scare, or it became a reality one day, how did you (or would you) cope?

Chapter 5

Hey, I Didn't Marry A Pastor!
Guiding Love: Helping Others To Find The Way

Recently a friend asked, "Did you realize what you were getting into when you became a preacher's wife?" Honestly, I don't remember not being a Pastor's wife, and then suddenly becoming one. It all happened so gradually...much like the boiling frog syndrome. You probably know the story. You can stick a frog into a pot of boiling water and he'll jump out immediately, knowing that it's hot and he's going to die. On the other hand, you can stick a frog into a pot of cold water and gradually turn up the heat until it comes to a boil. The frog doesn't realize it's getting hot until it's too late, so he dies because he never jumps. Although I've never done this experiment, and don't have plans to, my point is this—sometimes you don't realize what's happening until it's too late. This is what happened in my relationship with Larry. I definitely married the man I loved, but I didn't think I was marrying a Pastor...and I realized it into the process.

    This takes me back to John 16:12–13, because I believe God planned it that way. He had to guide me step by step in my spiritual growth, in order to prepare me for the ministry. I do remember Larry asking me if I thought being a preacher's wife was something I could handle. My response was if it meant I had to be someone I wasn't, I wouldn't want to be one. He respected that.

    Our God is a God of second chances, because Larry's been back in ministry for five

I have yet many things to say to you, but you cannot bear them now. When the Spirit of truth comes, he will guide you into all the truth; for he will not speak on his own authority, but whatever he hears he will speak, and he will declare to you the things that are to come.
Jn. 16:12–13, RSV

> Starting up the ministry came at a challenging time in our lives: when Larry and I were believing God to give us a child....God fulfilled our love by graciously allowing us to extend His love to others.

> But seek first His kingdom and His righteousness; and all these things shall be added to you. Therefore do not be anxious for tomorrow; for tomorrow will care for itself...
> Matt. 6:33–34

years! We started Fellowship of Plano in January 1998 with twelve people in a banquet room at a local Holiday Inn. Now we have a beautiful, red brick building with a green roof sitting on five acres of prime land smack dab in the middle of the city. Our membership has grown to three hundred fifty and we're in the process of building new facilities on our present acreage. Is God awesome or what? I'm really enjoying my walk with the Lord, and Larry has a peace about him now that I can't begin to explain.

Starting up the ministry came at a challenging time in our lives: when Larry and I were believing God to give us a child. It's like He gave us the grace to stand firm and say, "We trust You in all things, hope in all things, and can endure all things as we keep our hearts focused on You." And then He blessed us for it. Matthew 6:33 took on an entirely new meaning: We put God's kingdom first and established the church...then not long after, He blessed us with Luke. It was nothing less than a miracle. God fulfilled our love by graciously allowing us to extend His love to others.

Going Back To My Roots

I didn't have a strong religious background. My parents instilled great values in me and took us to church; but for me, it was merely a formality. We were Episcopalian, so I learned to genuflect beside each pew and recite the familiar phrases, "The Lord be with you...and also with you," and so on. I sat through the services because I had to. Every now and then, the church would sponsor fun events, but overall it bored me. I just didn't relate to it.

> My parents instilled great values in me and took us to church; but for me, it was merely a formality.

By the time I was out on my own, I'd developed a philosophy of life that was a far cry from religion or righteousness (I'll get to that later). Basically, I had head knowledge about God—as long as I attended church on Easter and Christmas, I felt that I'd done my good deed for the year. The rest of the time, I'd just try to be a "good person" and everything would be fine.

When I met Larry, I'd already learned that just trying to be a good person wasn't the answer—*nowhere near it*. I'd played out all my options. I was living on the edge, so I didn't get saved until I was in my thirties (I'd basically avoided church for eleven years!). I just never felt like I could step in a church and be myself. I guess that's why I have such a burden to be real. I wanted to make sure I could still be myself while functioning as a Pastor's wife. I didn't want to give up my personality and temperament and put on a spiritual mask—because putting on a mask covers the truth—and that doesn't help people come to God for help.

By the time I was out on my own, I'd developed a philosophy of life that was a far cry from religion or righteousness.

Where Do I Fit In?

Growing up, I had a problem with trying to fit in and cared deeply about what people thought about me. I tried to conform, especially as a teen. Now that I've worked through many issues in my life, being a Pastor's wife has put me in a unique position. I know that I live in a fishbowl and must be an excellent example—everybody's watching everything I do—yet I'm quite intent on being myself. I don't worry so much about people's opinions; I just stay true to who I am. And I don't try to conform to anything the public thinks I need to do or be in this position.

Each day, I do what I feel is right by the leading of God and the Holy Spirit. I like being different that way...just seeking to be pleasing in God's eyes. So in this sense, I can't care what others think I should be doing, because it would distract me from doing the Lord's work. I'd be too absorbed in things that aren't eternally important.

The story of King Saul comes to mind. First Samuel 8:19–22 says, "Nevertheless, the people refused to listen to the voice of Samuel, and they said, 'No, but there shall be a king over us, that we also may be like all the nations, that our king may judge us and go out before us and fight our battles.' Now after Samuel had heard all the words of the people, he repeated them in the LORD'S hearing. And the LORD said to Samuel, 'Listen to their voice, and appoint them a king...' "

The people wanted a king so they could be like everyone else (*a problem!*), and Saul was the perfect candidate, "...a choice and handsome {man,} and there was not a more handsome person than he among the sons of Israel; from his shoulders and up he was taller than any of the people" (1 Sam. 9:2). Saul ended up being a king who couldn't please God, because he was focused on man. Disobedience caused him to lose his kingdom.

" 'What have you done?' asked Samuel. Saul replied, 'When I saw that the men were scattering, and that you did not come at the set time, and that the Philistines were assembling at Micmash, I thought, Now the Philistines will come down against me at Gilgal, and I have not sought the LORD's favor. So I felt compelled to offer the burnt offering.' 'You acted foolishly,' Samuel said. 'You have not kept the command the LORD your God gave you; if you had, he would have established your kingdom over Israel for all time. But now your kingdom will not endure; the LORD has sought out a man after his own heart and appointed him leader of his people, because you have not kept the LORD's command' " (1 Sam. 13:11–14, NIV).

King Saul had the wrong focus. He wasn't looking toward heaven and the kingdom of God, so he tried to make things happen for himself. Like Saul, it would take all of my energy to be overly concerned with what people could do to hurt me. And if I keep my eyes on people, I won't be able to hear God and minister to them. So I've come to an important realization. I can only be the best person I can be, do the best job that I can, and make the best possible decisions under the guidance of the Holy Spirit. God started me in this process as a Pastor's wife, and I'm confident He'll be faithful to help me complete it.

The Challenge of Leadership

As a minister's wife, I knew I'd immediately be acknowledged as a leader. And I knew people would be coming to me for spiritual guidance. So from the beginning, I sensed an urgent need to seek the Lord with more intensity than ever. I knew that only Jesus was able to deal with my hidden issues and give me what I needed to minister alongside of Larry. I couldn't be passive about my faith. I had to spend time in prayer and study the Bible every day, *and that was just for starters.*

I also had to prepare myself to handle criticism. This is a vital part of seeking to please God instead of people. Not everybody likes you when you serve in a leadership position...and I knew I had to prepare myself to deal with criticisms constructively. People can be easily offended. I can stand up and smile in a room filled with people and offend someone without even realizing it. Therefore, I had to come to terms with the fact that everybody wasn't going to like me one hundred percent of the time, even in church. At times, I'd have to learn how to embrace being unpopular—but

> *{For I am} confident of this very thing, that He who began a good work in you will perfect it until the day of Christ Jesus.*
> Phil. 1:6

> *But without faith it is impossible to please Him, for he who comes to God must believe that He is, and that He is a rewarder of those who diligently seek Him.*
> Heb. 11:6, NKJ

> *I had to come to terms with the fact that everybody wasn't going to like me one hundred percent of the time, even in church.*

most of all, I'd have to be that Proverbs 31 woman, "She opens her mouth in wisdom, and the teaching of kindness is on her tongue" (vs. 26).

Another challenge is very specific to being a woman (and I think many women deal with this). That is, having the tendency to act like Superwoman and take too much upon myself. In ministry, this is incredibly easy to do, because there are always so many needs to be addressed. So I have to be careful. Before I know it, I'm sailing along thinking I can do it all, "Look at me! I can teach, write books, sing, do graduate studies, be a great mother..." and so on. In the meantime, my relationship with the Lord is starting to slip, my schedule with Luke is out of whack, I haven't seen Larry in a month, and I'm totally stressed out.

I had to identify the root issue: I can't do anything well if I'm trying to do everything. So I've learned how to be faithful in the little things (that I can handle) and then let God handle the big stuff (things I can't control). That's a huge lesson.

Sure, as a leader, I'll make mistakes. Every leader does. We can all make bad decisions or fail in some way—but we get back up again. That's what makes a good leader. We get back up, dust ourselves off, and go even further in the strength of the Lord.

The Social Challenge

Then there's the issue of friendships. I remember telling Larry that I needed friends outside of the church, because it's so easy to stay exclusively within the church framework. Usually, when people learn that I'm a pastor's wife, conversations gravitate to church topics; I end up inviting them to church, and so on. While this is wonderful, everyone needs a little

---

I had to identify the root issue: I can't do anything well if I'm trying to do everything.

For a righteous man falls seven times, and rises again, but the wicked stumble in {time of} calamity. Prov. 24:16

Sometimes I simply need to relax and be "Barb" with people I don't usually see in a church setting.

R&R. Sometimes I simply need to relax and be "Barb" with people I don't usually see in a church setting.

I generally don't tell people what I do when I'm socializing. A few years back, I played golf regularly with a group of women who didn't know I was a pastor's wife. We played and had a great time, and then somehow what Larry and I do slipped out. Immediately, things changed. Before they knew I was a preacher's wife, they were relaxed. They shouted when they hit a shot and cussed when they didn't. I just ignored them. We laughed and carried on. Afterwards, they tensed up. Every time one of the girls was about to say something that might offend me, she'd stop suddenly and apologize, "Oh my goodness, I'm so sorry I said that Barb...I didn't mean to..." I appreciated it, but I really didn't want to be treated differently than anyone else.

Another time, I went to a Pampered Chef party and one of the ladies was introducing me to the others, "This is Barbara Norrell..." I quickly turned to her and said, "Don't introduce me as a preacher's wife, please don't do it." Well, she accidentally said it, and sure enough (I could tell), the whole atmosphere in the room changed. There were eight or ten girls there, and when they heard I was a pastor's wife, it was like a dark cloud had descended upon them. Before they knew I was in the ministry, they were happily being themselves. Afterwards, it was almost as if nobody in the room could relax and enjoy the festivities. I could almost see them tensing up, thinking, "Oh no, I can't be myself. There's a preacher's wife in here..."

There's pressure involved in being a minister's wife. People look at you differently. To them, you live in a glass house and they expect perfection. And if they happen to see you fall short, they're quick to judge and

> *There's pressure involved in being a minister's wife. People look at you differently....I've longed for people to realize that I'm human, just like they are.*

criticize, because you're in a leadership position. *I've longed for people to realize that I'm human, just like they are.* I love what I do, but at times I may make a mistake—because no matter how much I love God and try to do what pleases Him, I'm not perfect! I pray every day, "Father, help me when I fall short because I know I will." And thankfully, He does.

Turning My "Burden" into Ministry

While employed at Southwest Airlines, I took quite a few courses on public speaking and developed one such course that was implemented throughout the company. A question students often asked was, "When I get up and talk in front of people, how should I talk to them?" My answer was, "Just talk to them like they're your best friend." If they were speaking to a group of 25,000, of course, they'd have to be more animated. The smaller the group, the more intimate they'd have to be. The bottom line is, whether you're working in corporate America or inside the church walls...people need to know you're real. That's when they respond, and when you can create an atmosphere where people will learn and grow.

> *The bottom line is, whether you're working in corporate America or inside the church walls...people need to know you're real.*

Being real is the whole concept for my women's group: *Reel to Real*, which I started in 1999—the same year I had Luke. Imagine how I adapted that name! I use movie titles and then apply a practical message each week from a biblical perspective. Mind you, the message is never about the movies. It's just fun to use the titles!

The group has been a great success. No one feels pressured to be anything she's not. Women from every walk of life feel free to come, learn, and openly share about what's most important to them. It still amazes me they keep coming back every week. And what a blessing we've been to each other through prayer, friendship, and our growth in the Lord.

Natural Versus Spiritual Principles

Ministry is about helping people, but I've also observed many similarities between ministries and secular organizations. That's right! A church operates much like a corporation and people act basically the same in ministry as they do in corporate America. The only difference is God, our common element—and thankfully, it does seem to make things easier. Leadership principles in ministry and business are also very similar. There is, however, one major difference.

When I worked in the corporate world, I was paid to teach, minister to, and counsel with people. Sometimes employees were required to take mandatory classes in order to be promoted. They didn't have any choice. In church, everything is done strictly on a volunteer basis. People willingly give their time and commitment without being paid a dime. This is truly incredible, a tangible testimony of their commitment to Christ and faithfulness to His mission.

As visionaries, Larry and I realize people don't always have the same level of vision and commitment as we do. Pastoring is what we do; Larry and I have a mutual passion to serve the Lord. It's our job. Yet we constantly reinforce the value of serving God and encourage people to get involved in the work of the ministry—because spiritual dividends far surpass anything in the earthly realm.

I Am Who I Am by The Grace of God

So how do I feel about being a Pastor's wife? Like it's totally from God, because it's a miracle that I'm alive and well, serving in the ministry with the man I love. Ten years ago, Larry and I were polar opposites. Anyone would have looked at us and said we weren't matched for marriage, much less ministry! I was into my career and partying the night away in every bar I could find, and Larry was a "Hell, fire, and brimstone" preacher who was literally trying to shut down every liquor store in town! Yes, if I ran into some of the people I used to know and told them I'm a preacher's wife, co-pastoring a church, singing on the praise team (*and loving every minute of it!*), they'd wonder what I'd been smoking—but now, that doesn't really matter.

No, I didn't think I was marrying a pastor, but I'm proud and blessed to be a pastor's wife! And though I could never serve in this capacity without God's help, I wouldn't change it for anything in the world.

> *I could never serve in this capacity without God's help, but I wouldn't change it for anything in the world.*

Reflections

1. God's timing isn't necessarily our timing. Can you identify an event in your life that was clearly on God's timetable?

2. What does Matthew 6:33, "But seek first His kingdom..." say to you?

3. Do you let "past traditions" keep you from growing in your life? Emotionally? Spiritually?

4. Do you long to be around people who are real? How do you rate in this regard?

Chapter 6

The Taste of The Pear

True Love: Seeing through Each Other's Eyes

Love sees what the eyes cannot. One of my favorite movies is *City of Angels* with Nicolas Cage and Meg Ryan. I especially love the scene where they're sitting in a market eating fruit and she bites into a pear. Nick's character looks at her and asks, "What does that taste like?" Surprised, she responds, "You don't know what a pear tastes like?" And he says, "I don't know what a pear tastes like to you." That line had such a profound impact on me because it touches an important issue in all relationships. We shouldn't assume anything about anyone, because a pear tastes different to every person.

We can assume a lot, "Well, my husband should know that..." or, "Doesn't he know that's how I am?" No, he usually doesn't! We can have so many unrealistic expectations. True love doesn't assume; it considers, communicates, and cooperates. Looking back on my relationship with Larry, we both have such a deep love for Christ, and for each other, because of the many challenges we've worked through. Each one has brought us through a process to reach the level of commitment we enjoy today.

Therefore, I can't ever assume I know everything Larry's thinking, because I don't know what a pear tastes like to him. And he can't assume he always knows what's on my heart. Thinking back, maintaining this perspective is what has kept our relationship going—it's kept our love alive.

We shouldn't assume anything about anyone, because a pear tastes different to every person.

True love doesn't assume; it considers, communicates, and cooperates.

Thinking back, this is what's kept our relationship going—it's kept our love alive.

A Woman's Tendency To Control

I fell in love with Larry exactly as he was. Yet it seemed that as soon as I'd fallen in love, I started taking advantage of him. This is scary. It's like the more love a woman feels for someone, the more we actually start taking things for granted and wanting to change him. We tend to think, "If he'd only be like this, he'd be better for me." Without realizing it, we're trying to take over God's job of molding the clay. We take the clay we thought was perfect in the beginning, and then start thinking, "He really needs to change...and I'm going to make sure it happens."

That's how most women look at our husbands! "I'm your hope, honey. I can change your hair...*let's see,* if you comb your hair back and put some gel in it, it would take years off your face. Honey, if you wear jeans, you'll look ten years younger..." Women are very controlling. We think we have all the answers, and that's why we're super women. We want to control everything: our husbands, kids, even trips to the grocery store.

I also realize that women can be tempted to control their husbands by using sex as a means of reward or punishment. This is unscriptural, but more than this, *it's just plain wrong*— because it's taking advantage of someone you love. Just imagine how you'd feel if your husband didn't communicate with you, or make you feel attractive, special, and loved: yet he expected you to be intimate on demand. It's selfish and unfair.

To me, the most important thing is communication. Sometimes I might want to make love and look over at Larry (sitting in his chair watching television) and say, "Hey, tonight's a good night, honey...Luke's in bed, are you in the mood?" He might say, "Yeah!" or he could say, "You know, Barb, I've had a rough day and have a lot on my mind. Could I take a rain check?" In other words, he lets me know that he's not just blowing me off. He makes sure to communicate his desire to reschedule. (I almost hate using the word, "reschedule" when referring to our sex life, but sometimes Larry and I have to be strategic.) After all, we have a three year old! Communicating about our desire to be intimate with each other is vitally important.

On the other hand, there have been times when Larry's asked me about making love, and I've responded the same way, "Could we set this up for another night? I've had a tough day being a mom to Luke and I'm tired..." I don't think there's anything wrong with this in a marriage. In general, I think as long as you talk openly and lovingly with your spouse, you'll have a wonderful sexual partnership.

There's nothing wrong with healthy sexual communication. It's part of life. Don't be intimidated by your partner, and don't be forced into any situation you don't want to be in...just talk to him. Tell him your needs, and discuss how you both can arrive at a solution. Larry and I do this often, "Let's take Luke to the babysitter and get a hotel room tomorrow..." Speak of solutions! Where there's a will, there's a way!

So don't just blow off your spouse; this can cause misunderstanding and resentment, and plant seeds of rejection. Too often, women don't communicate effectively when it comes to sex and try to control their husbands. I believe this is why some men end up having affairs with their secretaries. Let me explain. Secretaries are "yes" people. All a man has to do is ask, "Would you get me a cup of coffee?" "Yes, sir." "Would you copy these papers for me?" "Yes, sir. I'd love to..." The secretary is simply earning a living, but to a man her demeanor communicates respect—and that can definitely lead to trouble if there are relationship problems at home.

Taste The Pear

Considering the challenges that Larry and I have overcome, the biggest thing I've learned is to try looking at things through his eyes whenever I can. Realistically, I know I won't always be able to do so—but if I truly stop being selfish, I could start wanting to do things *for him* instead of trying to control him. If I haven't walked a mile in Larry's shoes, how can I possibly know what he needs? Women could save a lot of heartaches in our relationships if we try looking at things the way our spouses would.

Unless women stay close to God and keep our eyes on Him, we can easily misuse our God-given ability to nurture. This innate capacity we have to process and take care of many things at once can turn into manipulation if we're not careful.

For example, when Larry comes home, he loves to hug. Actually, we both do. When he returns after a weeklong hunting trip, though, I'm usually ready to do more. I want to spend some quality time with him. And I could be taking bites out of my own pear thinking of how I'm going to say, "I've missed you, honey...I want to spend time with you tonight," and then make sure everything's in place to make it happen. I could fix a romantic dinner, put Luke to bed early, and so on, just relishing the prospect of our intimate evening. The problem occurs when I do it without considering how Larry's going to feel when he gets home (or talking to him while he's en route and asking what he thinks).

Let's say the scene plays out. Larry comes in, falls into a chair, and picks up the remote control. He's tired. He just wanted to get home and rest—but I've orchestrated everything for a romantic encounter. Now, I'm ready for an argument. I could accuse him of taking my patience and hard work for granted; but in actuality, nothing could be further from the truth! I had an unrealistic expectation of him. Larry had no idea what I was putting together at home. The thought never entered his mind that we were supposed to have a romantic evening. And in this scenario, since I didn't communicate with him beforehand, Larry walked into a trap.

In reality, I know that nothing is likely to happen between us the first night Larry returns from a hunting trip! By considering his needs, I don't expect him to do anything but rest. And I enjoy having him back, even if he falls asleep in front of the television! We have plenty of time to be together. What's most important is that he's safely at home. I've learned that by treating Larry the way I know he needs to be treated (the way I treated him when we first met), he continues to amaze me in the wonderful things he does for me!

I've learned that by treating Larry the way I know he needs to be treated (the way I treated him when we first met), he continues to amaze me in the wonderful things he does for me!

The Danger of Unrealistic Expectations

When women have unrealistic expectations of our spouse, we try to change him. I believe this is the root cause of most marriage problems today—people are constantly trying to change each other. There were times early in our marriage that Larry tried to make me behave a certain way, and I did the same to him. I believe most couples have to work through this during their first few years of marriage, and it can be extremely difficult.

I believe the root cause of most marriage problems today is that people are constantly trying to change each other.

On the other hand, I've talked to people that have been married twenty, twenty-five, or thirty years and they've told me, "We've grown to know each other so well, we don't let the little things get to us anymore. It's just not worth it." I saw on television recently that the divorce rate in the United States is at fifty-eight percent and climbing. To me, this only proves what the Bible teaches.

Mark 10:8–9 says, " '...they are no longer two, but one flesh. Therefore what God has joined together, let not man separate' " (NKJ). Ecclesiastes 4:9–12 confirms, "Two are better than one, because they have a good reward for their labor. For if they fall, one will lift up his companion. But woe to him who is alone when he falls, for he has no one to help him up....Though one may be overpowered by another, two can withstand him. And a threefold cord is not quickly broken" (NKJ). We cannot expect to have successful marriages unless God is the center of our relationship.

Believers have the same marital challenges as unbelievers. When Christ is the center of a marriage, we can learn and grow. If not, we tend to get out of it. For a lot of people, it's easier to give up. Then they have to face other problems, like who gets the house, who will get custody of the kids, and so on. They get centered on all of these things and then start freaking out about it—but I truly believe if people would just try putting their focus on God, He could restore many things.

Having unrealistic expectations can be disastrous. It's like looking at our spouse's weaknesses through a magnifying glass and our own through rose-colored lenses. Unrealistic expectations almost cost Larry and me our marriage in the early years. I can remember at least two or three times when we looked at each other and said, "This was a mistake...let's just

---

Believers have the same marital challenges as unbelievers. When Christ is the center of a marriage, we can learn and grow. If not, we tend to get out of it.

Having unrealistic expectations is like looking at our spouse's weaknesses through a magnifying glass and our own through rose-colored lenses.

get out of it." I'm so thankful to the Lord we didn't give up.

The Need for Sacrifice

Love requires sacrifice, and it takes work to sacrifice in our marriages. If we're really honest with ourselves, we'd admit that we don't like to work. Most people would prefer six days of entertainment and one day of effort. Couples want to have instant marriages. Face it. We want instant everything! First Corinthians 13:4 says, "Love suffers long and is kind..." (NKJ). It takes time and patience to build a strong relationship.

Human beings are impatient. If we don't get what we want *right now*, then we're unhappy. The fact is: we all have gold deep inside our hearts, but it takes work to mine it. First, we have to find it. Then we have to dig for it...and that's why some people never reach their potential. They have to put forth an earnest effort in order to reap the benefits! I don't want somebody mining my gold for me, and then giving me a mere percentage. I want to learn about mining myself; understand how to go about it. It might take years, but I'm willing to invest the time that's needed to reap all of the benefits.

In my relationship with Larry, this means I'm willing to sacrifice now to build a solid future with him. For instance, I set up coffee every night on an automatic timer to brew the following morning. I just love the way it smells as I'm walking down the hall to the kitchen...it's a great wake up call! One day, Larry woke up about 30 minutes before me and was sitting in the den reading the paper when I arrived. I noticed the coffee pot was still full and thought, "Why hasn't he gotten any coffee? He's waiting for me to get it for him." So instead of getting

Human beings are impatient. If we don't get what we want right now, then we're unhappy. The fact is: we all have gold deep inside our hearts, but it takes work to mine it.

upset and assuming he was taking me for granted, I asked, "Larry, can I get you a cup of coffee this morning?"

As it turned out, Larry wasn't waiting for me to get his coffee; he'd just forgotten to get a cup before he started reading the paper. To him, it didn't matter if he poured a cup for himself, or if I poured it for him. He wasn't waiting for me to serve him...and if he was, what's so bad about that? Jesus said, "For even the Son of Man did not come to be served, but to serve, and to give His life a ransom for many" (Mk. 10:45). I love Larry. It makes me happy to serve him, and I know he feels the same way about me. If I can pour a cup of coffee for Larry, it's just one, small opportunity to show him how much he means to me.

Larry and I have learned not to assume there's a hidden agenda if we have a misunderstanding. Instead, we've learned to ask, "What can I do for you?"

When we counsel couples with marital problems, I often say, "Don't give up. There was a reason you married each other, and you have to get back to it. *Get back to when you met.* Try to remember how you felt about each other at *that* time, because if even one of you can try to work this out, there's hope..."

When Larry and I were in the thick of dealing with his trust issue, he said to me one day, "Barb, this is my problem. It's my insecurity. The thing you can do to help me through it is to understand I'm falling short in this area." From that point on, I learned to hear him out. I may not have always agreed with what he was saying, but I listened. I could have easily continued to treat his problem with disdain. After all, it wasn't my issue.

Sometimes there's nothing more dangerous than trying to be right. Too many times, we get angry and think, "That's *your* problem. That's

> *I learned to hear him out. I may not have always agreed with what he was saying, but I listened.*

> *My job as a wife and his job as a husband are the same: to understand, help, and support each other.*

your insecurity. Deal with it!" This attitude is wrong! Marriage is a commitment, and there are many levels of sacrifice. Now that Larry and I have learned to *taste the pear*, we understand what we need to do. My job as a wife and his job as a husband are the same: to understand, help, and support each other. In doing this, we're living in obedience to the Lord and building a bright, wonderful future.

Larry and I aren't perfect, but I'm so thankful God has helped us to overcome in our marriage. We've faced many storms, but as we kept our eyes on the Lord, keeping His kingdom principles first—our marriage has continued to get better with time. I can truly say Larry and I have learned to *taste the pear* in our relationship. We've learned to see through each other's eyes. And in the years to come, I trust and pray our love story will become a family legacy.

Reflections

1. In what ways do you try to view things from someone else's perspective? Is it hard for you to do? Do you assume or have unrealistic expectations of your spouse or mate?

2. Do you find yourself trying to control some situations? What usually happens if they're beyond your control? Which emotions do you experience? What are the results?

3. Sacrifice is hard. That's why it's called *sacrifice*. Can you remember a time when you sacrificed to get what you wanted?

Part II

A Place Called "There"

The lamp of the body is the eye; if therefore your eye is clear, your whole body will be full of light. But if your eye is bad, your whole body will be full of darkness. If therefore the light that is in you is darkness, how great is the darkness! No one can serve two masters; for either he will hate the one and love the other, or he will hold to one and despise the other. You cannot serve God and mammon. For this reason I say to you, do not be anxious for your life, {as to} what you shall eat, or what you shall drink; nor for your body, {as to} what you shall put on. Is not life more than food, and the body than clothing?

Matthew 6:22–25

Chapter 7

I'm Outta Here!

Frustrated Love: Escaping The Ideal Family

It's so important to get a good start in life, because the way we begin can determine our final outcome. My earliest memories of my biological mother are sketchy. She was gone a lot, so my dad and I spent a lot of time together, and he did most of the cooking. Such was my early life—until one night when everything changed. I remember sitting on a barstool in my parents' apartment eating macaroni and cheese—my favorite meal (and the only one dad cooked well!). My mother walked into the room with a couple of suitcases and said, "I'm leaving you, John."

I was about three years old at the time, so I didn't understand what was going on. I remember thinking, "Where's mommy going? Why does she have suitcases?" And then she was gone. I didn't see or talk to her again until many years later.

As I grew older, I never asked dad about what happened that night. It remained a quiet subject. We just put the past behind us, and dad started to rebuild our lives. We became very close. To me, my dad is the most amazing man in the world—aside from Larry, that is. I love and respect him deeply. He was my first Prince Charming, my original hero.

I can still remember, though, seeing mannequins at the mall and thinking, "Oh, she's so beautiful..." So I'd stop my dad and say, "Dad, this is the one. I want this one to be my mom." I know it probably broke his heart. I was

It's so important to get a good start in life, because the way we begin can determine our final outcome.

A Place Called "There" / Frustrated Love: Escaping The Ideal Family

> *I can still remember seeing mannequins at the mall and thinking, "Oh, she's so beautiful..." So I'd stop my dad and say, "Dad, this is the one. I want this one to be my mom."*

just too young to understand. Childishly, I thought we could just pick out a "new mom" at the store, and I wanted her to be the prettiest, most gorgeous one. Beauty was always a big deal to me.

Interestingly, my biological mother had been very beautiful. She was a Playboy Bunny in Chicago, where I was born. Years later, I learned that she was given an opportunity to work in a new Playboy club in Jamaica. That's when she left us.

Our New Family

I didn't realize that a "real person" could end up marrying my dad, but that's what happened. A few years later, he married a wonderful woman named Jan. She lived close by and took care of me every now and then. Actually, she didn't start out liking him. She liked me...so she'd ask my dad if she could take me places. Thinking back, Jan really had affection for me and that's what brought them together. After they married, they had two daughters of their own. Valorie came first, followed by Teresa two years later.

> *I was living in a dream world, never certain why my biological mother had left me, and somehow always feeling like an outsider.*

I lived in this wonderful, middle class family until I graduated from high school, and was very loved. Still, hidden layers of resentment from my past kept resurfacing. I was living in a dream world, never certain why my biological mother had left me, and somehow always feeling like an outsider. I developed a "Cinderella complex" early on, thinking I was always being singled out and treated unfairly. Nothing could have been further from the truth, but that was my perception.

One thing that always impressed me about my parents is they never spoke badly about my biological mother. They didn't lie about the situation, *I just knew of her*. My parents didn't want me to form my opinions based on what *they thought.* I love and appreciate them for this.

By my teenage years, rebellion was in full bloom. It was obvious that I wasn't happy. I convinced myself that when I graduated from high school, I was out of there. And that's exactly what I did—only I left the wrong way, and I paid dearly for it. I'll get to that later.

Jan was an excellent mother and the family disciplinarian. That was hard for me, because I'd always been "daddy's little girl"—his special, little child—the firstborn from his first wife. During my entire life, he'd only spanked me once when I was about five years old. I remember it vividly. I was sitting in the bathroom one day and decided to squirt toothpaste all over the mirror and the wall. Dad came in, spanked me on the behind...*and I was devastated!* How could my Prince Charming do such a thing?

Jan (whom I lovingly refer to as mom) was quite different. I'll never forget when I was twelve or thirteen and did something at the breakfast table that really made her mad. Afterwards, I grabbed my purse, said, "I'm going to school..." and pranced out the door. To my astonishment, mom came running after me with a broom! "You come back here right now, I'm not done with you!" To make matters worse, all of my friends were walking to the bus stop, so they saw everything. No, mom didn't hit me with the broom—but she definitely got my attention.

An Ideal Upbringing

Mom taught me many things, but above all else, she taught me how to be my own person. She showed me how to be independent. Luke's even benefited from mom's ethic: He's so independent, and I love that about him! When I try to put socks on him, he says, "Mommy, I can do it myself." I try to brush his teeth and he interrupts, "Mommy, I can do it myself!" I know Luke's independence will give him the strength and drive he'll need to achieve his goals. No matter how challenging it may be, he'll see it through. I have mom to thank for that—because she gave me this most precious gift.

Mom was always cognizant of money; extremely careful with what my dad worked hard to earn for our household. She even made our clothes (though sometimes I hated it). When I was a pre-teen, I remember her making a swimming suit for me that I thought was just awful. All my other friends were wearing bikinis and I had to wear this homemade suit that wasn't in style. I remember hiding in the pool because I was so embarrassed. Mom and I laugh about it now, but then, I was horrified.

She was very nurturing; an excellent mother. For starters, without fail she cooked a nutritious breakfast for us every morning because she'd read somewhere that children learn better when they have something warm in their stomachs. Mom never told us to get the cereal box—that was for Saturdays. She did economize by serving powdered milk, though. It was my job on Sunday nights to mix it up for the following week. I hated powdered milk!

Dad and mom really worked well together. Yes, they were careful with money, but we still had a nice family vacation every summer and a wonderful Christmas each year. I'll never forget asking Santa to bring me white, leather go-go boots when I was ten. On Christmas morning, there they were under the tree...*I was ecstatic*. I know mom had a big part in making it happen.

She was also an expert at home remedies. In high school, I got a really bad case of athlete's foot; but I didn't tell mom about it. One night, though, she saw my foot and had a fit.

She immediately prepared something called a hot poultice by combining bread, milk, and some other ingredients on the stove and then wrapping it around my foot. She said it was supposed to fight infections. A few days later, when we returned to the doctor, he said that mom could have saved my foot. Before this, they'd actually been thinking it might become necessary to amputate a couple of toes.

Early Stages of Pressing The Envelope

On another occasion, I think mom probably saved my life. From an early age, I had a tendency to test the limits by doing extremely adventurous, even dangerous, things—with absolutely no thought of the consequences. When I was around ten or eleven years old, we were living in a new residential area in Houston. Across the street from us, a nice home was being built that had two-story scaffolding set up in front. *It was irresistible.* Before long, a friend and I were jumping out of the second floor window like trapeze artists—hanging on the bars, flipping, and having a great time...until mom saw us from the kitchen window. I'll never forget seeing her run across the front yard, wooden spoon in hand, screaming, "Barbara Gayle, get down off of that thing!" Thank God she stopped us before we had a serious accident.

Mom also had a lighter side. I can remember a time when I was spending the night with my best friend, Janice, and we decided to make prank calls. We were laughing and having lots of fun, and then I got on the phone (stupid me!) and dialed my home phone number by mistake...at 2:00 in the morning! When mom answered, I didn't recognize her voice. I said, "Janice..." (I was using my friend's name, but it just happened to be mom's name as well!) My mom said, "Yes?" Before I knew it, she had me pegged, "Barbara Gayle, get off of that phone!"

I remember thinking, "Did my mom just walk in the room?" And then I realized she was on the telephone! I just hung up, thinking, "I can't go home in the morning." I couldn't sleep. I was petrified all night. The next day, when I walked in the house, mom was sitting there looking stern...and then started laughing so hard she couldn't stop. She didn't punish me; I guess I'd hit a funny bone.

Still, I was aching inside from my early abandonment. I became so headstrong that I rebelled every time mom told me I couldn't do something I wanted to do. I'd spit out at her accusingly, "You're telling me I can't do that because you just don't like me, because I'm not your *real* daughter. You're picking me out! You're just doing this because I'm not your real blood. If my real mother were here, she'd let me do it!" I was so unfair to her; I bucked everything she said.

Rebellion was my way of escaping the real issues. It amazes me that for at least five or six years, I lived in that Cinderella dream world. It was easy to think, "Poor me, I have a stepmother and two stepsisters..." because I could contend *with them* daily. I couldn't begin to imagine how to come to terms with the early rejection of my biological mother. So I rejected the only mother I knew, selfishly resisting her guidance and refusing to do anything she asked of me. Other times, I'd disobey and then blatantly tell a lie when confronted.

Around the seventh or eighth grade, my parents got me braces. I couldn't do anything about the hardware on my teeth, but I was dead set against wearing that awful headgear. I remember mom saying, "You listen to the doctor and wear that headgear to school, because we've spent all this money to fix your teeth..." I didn't care. I wasn't going to school with a wire around my head! So each day, she'd send me out to the bus stop with the headgear on. At the bus stop, I'd quickly take it out. Then when I got off the bus in the afternoon, I'd put it back on before walking home. Mom would ask, "Have you worn that all day?" Without blinking, I'd say, "Yeah!"

One night when I was about fifteen, I lost control. My parents had gone out and left us with our grandmother. I'd ended up watching Valorie and Teresa all night and was getting frustrated. Then Teresa (about six or seven years old at the time) made me mad about something, so I threw her into a door and it split her head open. I'll never forget seeing the impact; it was like watching slow motion. She hit the top of the door and then slid down, her body seemingly glued to the surface. Blood was everywhere.

It was one of the most panicked moments of my life. I thought, "Oh my gosh, I've killed my sister!" Then she started screaming...and strangely, I felt a sudden surge of relief, "Okay, I haven't killed her. She's still alive! Thank goodness!" In the meantime, Valorie was screaming, "What did you do to Teresa?" When our parents got home, they rushed her to the Emergency Room, and everything worked out. I thank God Teresa's okay.

Of course, I went through the natural "big sister" problems, like coming home and seeing my little sisters stare through the window as I kissed my date goodnight. Valorie and Teresa were intrigued with my boyfriends. I remember them doing gymnastics in the front yard—*like my dates really cared!* The girls were just showing off, being kids, but it was so embarrassing for me as a teenager. I remember thinking, "Why do I have these younger sisters?"

Early Family Responsibilities

While we were living in Houston, dad had taught me how to mow the yard. I loved mowing the lawn! By the time we moved to Hurst, Texas (when I was about twelve years old), I was taking great pride in my work. I'd actually walk down the block and look back at our house, thinking, "What a wonderful job I've done!" Dad and I kept our yard looking good. He'd fertilize it, and later, I'd mow it to perfection. We called ourselves "the yard people." It was almost like therapy for me...and was the beginning of my great love for the outdoors.

As you probably picked up from my flying trapeze incident in Houston, I was somewhat of a tomboy. So dad was smart to direct my energies toward mowing the lawn—at least that kept me on the ground! By the time I entered high school, I started running and earned the ninth grade track award. That's when my athleticism really began. I loved to run. I ran throughout my high school years; then in my early twenties, I started hitting the race circuit.

I ran so many 5K and 10K races that my knees are now beginning to feel the effects. A lot of those races were on concrete, which over the long term, has caused some cartilage damage. I did enjoy myself, though. And I never did superbly well, but I wasn't at the end of the pack, either. I was always in the middle, which in turn, reminded me of my high school days.

At fifteen, I started working at my dad's restaurant (Della's Café) in Grapevine, Texas. It was about thirty minutes from our home in Hurst, down a little road called Business Highway 121. I started out as a dishwasher and then at sixteen, graduated to waitress. I have so many great memories of that time in my life. On the days I worked, my dad woke me up early in the morning. He'd get us coffee and we'd leave home at about 4:30 a.m. In another hour, dad had to be in the restaurant making biscuits in order to open for business by 6:00 a.m. We never talked much during our drives to work, it was too early—*but just being with him was special.*

My parents really developed me. They both did such a wonderful job of influencing me in the right way, especially knowing what I needed to overcome. I definitely had some rough points, but thanks to great parents, I started early developing the practical tools for a successful life.

Dangerous Decisions

My job at the restaurant actually paved the way for the second time my father disciplined me. I was about sixteen and there was a cook at the restaurant that my dad trusted to bring me home in case I had to work a little later than he did. One evening, I was waiting tables and a nice looking, twenty-one year old asked me if I'd like to go out with him sometime. Naïvely, I said, "Sure!" Then the night came. Dad had left earlier and asked Rusty to bring me home.

To make a long story short, I let the twenty-one year old take me home instead of Rusty. While we were driving, he said, "Let's stop by the lake on our way." I agreed. I could have easily been abducted, raped, or killed! We ended up just kissing, and then he took me home (actually, I made him drop me off four houses from where we lived so my parents wouldn't see his car).

When I walked in the door, my father was standing there with a look on his face I'll never forget. He knew exactly what had happened (I guess Rusty had called him)—and was waiting for me. His bottom lip was shaking. He picked me up by the collar and said, "Where have you been?" I started crying, "I'm sorry, I'm sorry..." Then he put me down and said, "You get to your room, I don't even want to talk to you right now." He was really upset.

I can only imagine what it would be like to know your child is out there somewhere doing something stupid, and you can't do anything about it. The torment I must have put him through! I remember he came in my room later and said, "You don't know what you did to me tonight." I'd never seen my father like that. So many things could have happened that didn't. When I think of it now, I know God was protecting me.

Then there were the cigarettes. That same year, I decided to pursue my curiosity for smoking...and finally, the perfect opportunity came. My parents were planning to have a party, so I thought it would be the best time to learn the fundamentals. Somehow I'd gotten someone to buy me a pack of Marlboro's, and when my parents were busy with the party I snuck out to the garage and climbed into my dad's brown Pinto station wagon. I began lighting up one cigarette after another trying to inhale each one until I'd gone through the entire pack. I must have been in that car for three hours! When I finally came out, I opened the car door and smoke billowed everywhere.

I felt sick to my stomach. I made it back to the house, and then heard my mom calling to me, "Honey, I'd like you to meet..." There was no way. I remember saying, "I can't do that right now," and then I barely made it to the bathroom where I threw up. Strangely, that sour experience didn't curb my desire to smoke. *Smoking was forbidden, and that made it very alluring.* So I snuck around and smoked whenever I could. Sadly, this developed into a lifelong cycle of smoking, quitting, and then smoking again. I can still remember telling my mom, "I'm going to pull weeds in the back yard," and then I'd go all the way to the back fence to sneak a cigarette. Whose daughter pulls weeds? I wasn't fooling anyone.

Other times, I'd come home from school and put down my purse only to have mom confront me with the question, "Have you been smoking?" "No," I'd answer matter-of-factly. The problem was that she could smell it on me! So she'd pour out the contents of my purse right in front of me and let the cigarettes fall on the counter. *That still didn't shake me.* After getting my driver's license, I'd drive dad's car to the grocery store just to sneak cigarettes...until they caught me, that is. One day, they showed up at the store and found me sitting in the parking lot, lighting up.

The Rewards of Responsibility

Another thing that got to me was mom insisting on being involved in what I did with my paychecks. Every time I brought a paycheck home, she'd take some of the money. She'd say, "How much did you make?" and I'd tell her. "Okay, you get to keep one third, and I'm taking the rest." I used to get so mad! After all, it was *my money.* I was working hard and wanted to buy teen clothes and bell-bottoms..." I protested, but mom would explain, "Barb, I just want to help you save. I want to show you what saving's about..."

She never told me they were using that money to help save for my first car! My mom was so frugal. She and dad had already decided they could afford to pay half for a good, used car that was just a few years old. So she took the money I earned, put it with hers, and then one day not long after I'd gotten my driver's license they came to me and said, "Barb, we've got a surprise for you."

It was a non-incidental day; it wasn't even my birthday. They just said, "We want you to come out and look at something in the driveway." I said, "Well...okay." When I walked outside, I saw a sporty little 1971 Toyota SX sitting there waiting for me! It was yellow and had a big bow tied around it. They beamed, "This is for you." And then the best part came..."You paid for half of it." I was totally beside myself, "I did?" "Yes. Do you remember the money we were taking from your paychecks? Well, you purchased half of your own car."

I remember feeling a wonderful sense of ownership. What an incredible gift! I took pride in maintaining it. I can't help but think I wouldn't have valued it nearly as much if they'd bought it with their own money. Now, I was an owner. That made the car even more special. So I kept it clean and gassed up, changed the oil, and took care of it to the best of my ability. My father had always told me, "Take care of your things," so I did. My parents taught me so many, incredible principles.

A Costly Mistake

Still, I couldn't wait to get out of the house and do exactly as I pleased. And that didn't include going to college. How grieved my parents must have been! As much as they'd loved and guided me through life, I perceived it as control. To me, they were too strict. So by the time I was a senior in high school (in 1977–78), my mind was made up. Finally, I was going to do things my own way.

On the first day of school that year, I met Keith. We became buddies and just knew we'd get married someday. That became part of my exit plan. Right after I graduated at the age of seventeen, I moved out and got my own apartment. Keith got an apartment in the same complex. We didn't want to live together, we knew that was wrong, so we lived there and dated until my twenty-first birthday. Then we got married.

My parents had offered to send me to college, and I hadn't been a bad student in high school. I just didn't enjoy school because I was into the rebellious scene. Later, as I walked down the aisle, I can still remember thinking..."Why am I doing this?"...but I didn't stop. There were 150 people waiting to see me get married—*why look bad?* I was a beautiful bride. And when I walked in, everybody stood up and was looking at me. I remember walking and thinking, "This is the biggest mistake of my life, but they're all looking. So we'll go through with it and just make it work. I'll work it out."

I was so misguided. It was almost like I'd come to the conclusion, "If we get divorced, it will be worth it to save face. We can't let all of these people go home, and quit this marriage ceremony. This will be worth all of the headaches later." Again, that was far from reality. What's scary is, I've talked to countless women that have said the exact same thing. Take a word of advice. If you have doubts when you're walking down the aisle, *stop then.* To heck with anyone who doesn't understand. They don't have to live your life! You do! If you change your mind, all they can do is go home and say the wedding was called off. No big deal, right?

I convinced myself everything would work out and my dreams would eventually come true. Keith was going to carry me away into a new, fairytale existence.

I found out, however, life away from home involved many more responsibilities. I had to

If you have doubts when you're walking down the aisle, stop then. To heck with anyone who doesn't understand. They don't have to live your life! You do!

support myself. And then I got married and had to learn how to make a life with someone else. It was a far cry from dating—and I wasn't ready for it! I didn't even know myself, much less how to be in a successful marital relationship. Life turned out to be nothing like what I'd dreamed. For me, it was a total letdown.

Yet this experience wasn't for nothing. It brought me to a new level of awareness, even though *Cinderella* was still whispering in the recesses of my mind. Dissatisfied, I thought, "Someday, I'll meet my Prince." That wasn't going to happen for many years...in the meantime, I had a lot more growing to do.

Reflections

1. Almost all of us have disliked our parents at some point while growing up. Can you recall a really funny moment, where in hindsight, you now say, "My parents did a good thing"?

2. Has anyone you've loved let you down in such a way that you carried the scars for a long time? If so, do you still carry this burden, or have you healed? How did you get through it?

3. Feeling abandoned, neglected, and lonely is such an "empty" experience. Have you ever felt empty inside as a result of these emotions?

4. Repercussions of a painful past can last a lifetime. For instance, with me it was abandonment (so when I was older, I'd leave men before they had a chance to leave me). What if this painful past was clearly not your fault, as with me? Has this ever happened to you, and if so, how did you cope? Even if you couldn't change a situation, were you able to put it to rest in your heart?

Chapter 8

Oh Happy Day

Misdirected Love: A Journey in Self Discovery

I'd always been an attractive child, just not what I considered to be really pretty. I was tall, thin, and had legs up to my neck. So I felt average. I'd attended a large high school (in a graduating class of about 750 students), yet as I said before, I always found myself in the middle. I didn't hang out with the unpopular crowd, nor did I manage to get in with the real popular kids. My biggest achievement in high school (other than the track award) came during my junior year when I began dating one of the football players. He wasn't one of the most popular players—like the quarterback—but he was on the football team. To me, that was impressive.

I went through the early years never quite measuring up to my own "mannequin" standard of beauty. In fact, I didn't think most men considered me to be attractive until about a year into my marriage. I was working as a secretary in a bank when, suddenly, I became aware that men were starting to notice me. I remember them coming into the lobby, and to my surprise, I was getting "looks!" Some even approached me telling me how attractive I was.

I started telling myself, "Well, maybe I'm getting prettier...maybe I'm doing something right." So I thought, "Oh Happy Day! Let me work on this." I started dressing really cute, styling my hair, and working on my makeup. I liked the attention.

I've always dressed a little on the funky side, different...somewhat on the edge. My sisters and family would make fun of the way I dressed. I believe it's partly because I wasn't allowed to wear certain clothes growing up. I couldn't wear jeans to school, was forced to wear homemade bathing suits, and so on. So when I got away from home and got married, I felt like I'd been liberated. I started going for it.

This created a serious problem in my marriage. I'd become attractive to other men, and to be honest with you, I was looking at my husband thinking, "You don't see me like *they* do. You're still stuck in high school." My perception was skewed, because Keith really loved me. The problem was; I didn't love him the way a wife should love her husband.

Immature Infatuation

In looking back, I think Keith was too immature for me and I was too immature for marriage. I felt unattractive in high school, so marrying my buddy seemed to be the best I could do. I thought, "I'd better go ahead and do it." On the other hand, I believe Keith really cared for me. He seemed to dote on me, in a way. So in retrospect, I was thinking, "I probably won't ever find anybody like this, so I'll settle for what I can have, rather than what I really want."

In all honesty, I wasn't satisfied with our relationship from the beginning, because I still remember thinking, "Why am I doing this?" as I walked down the aisle on our wedding day. Against my gut feeling, I convinced myself it would ultimately work out. I discovered, however, this was an unrealistic expectation. I was too immature. And my heart just wasn't in it.

Maybe Keith gave me the security I needed to get out of the house and finally gain the independence I so desperately wanted. What's so strange about it is, we'd waited several years before getting married; we were already independent as individuals and enjoying each other's companionship. So when I think back, maybe we got married simply because we'd been saying we would for years. Maybe we married out of obligation, or because it just seemed like the thing to do.

Then, of course, we'd told people about it, committed to it. Above everything else, I think that was probably the biggest factor for me: meeting what I perceived to be other people's expectations. I didn't want us to fail in our decision, that is, look like a failure to others. What a snare! And this is a problem for many people: We want to save face and always come out looking good...*especially* if we've been rejected or abandoned.

Keith was the first man I'd ever been intimate with, but there were times when I dreaded it, because I didn't feel that intimacy connection. That was a big sign. I thought the world of Keith, but I didn't love him. I can remember thinking at times, "Oh gosh, I don't want to do this..." when we were about to make love. Keith didn't deserve that.

If you're really in love, *you'll know it.* And I wasn't. The bottom line is, Keith and I were great friends and communicators. In this respect, we were good for each other. We did a lot of fun things together; we even had neighbors in our apartment complex that we'd play cards and board games with until all hours of the night...we just weren't meant to be married.

The Affair

At work, I continued to enjoy the attention I was getting from other men. And I was starting to think I was just a little too cute, and maybe a little too good for what I had at home. I was

> *I didn't want us to look like a failure to others. What a snare! And this is a problem for many people: We want to save face ...especially if we've been rejected or abandoned.*

starting to think, "Maybe there's something out there that might be better for me." This brought about the demise of our relationship. I met a man that I began seeing and became unfaithful to Keith. What basically happened is that I had an affair and then told Keith about it because I couldn't live with myself—and that's what ended our marriage.

The man I had an affair with was also married, which made the situation even worse. What a terrible thing to do! But we were both young and obviously not mature enough to understand our marital commitments. They were supposed to be for life! And that's a long time, at least 50–60 years! *When we're young, we don't have a real concept of time.* Heart disease seems to be as far away as retirement...we think we're invincible—but nothing could be further from the truth.

The affair was exciting and new, much like the verbal attention I'd been getting at the office. Added to that, we were sneaking around, which seemed to enhance the appeal. I found out later, though, that intimacy and sex can be truly awesome when shared with somebody you love. It's more of a head-thing than anything. Physically, everybody does it the same way...so the difference is what you feel for that person, what you want to do for that person.

So there I was, definitely misguided and on the wrong track. Initially, I'd thought, "I've found myself again," but that proved to be wrong. I had to admit my unfaithfulness to my husband. When I did, Keith was amazingly willing to forgive and forget what had happened and keep moving forward in our marriage. I think he could have had some idea something was going on, because he handled the news so well. Unconsciously, though, I was looking for a way out. So my immediate reaction was, "What a wimp!" From the day Keith forgave me, I started to lose respect for him...and it gradually expanded to almost every area of our relationship—but believe me, it was more my problem than his.

Now, I'd think, "What a great thing!" God tells us to forgive. He's also told us we're going to fall short sometimes and make mistakes. The most successful preachers in the world make mistakes! Men and women of God in the Bible made mistakes—but if we can forgive, *great power is released.* It's called redemption: gaining something that's been lost. When I think back on it, Keith was doing the most godly thing a man could do. He did such a blessed thing when he was willing to forgive and go on. What a man of integrity and character!

Still, our marriage didn't work out. I just couldn't do it anymore. I was too immature for marriage and I'd gone too far to turn back. I actually remember thinking at the time Keith forgave me, "Well dang, now what do I have to do?" The sad fact was *I was ready to get out of the marriage.* And I'd reached the point where I was willing to acknowledge to anyone that I was wrong to get married in the first place.

Sharing My Mistake

My biggest fear was telling my parents. "How am I ever going to tell them?" I wondered, "They're going to think I'm the biggest loser in the world." What actually happened was quite different, however, and such a credit to my mother. I didn't have the heart to tell dad, so I invited mom to lunch at Steak & Ale, planning to tell her everything—and I'll never forget it. We had just ordered our meal. I leaned across the table and said, "Mom, there's something I need to tell you and it's laying real heavily on me." She looked at me with very concerned eyes and

Men and women of God in the Bible made mistakes— but if we can forgive, great power is released. It's called redemption: gaining something that's been lost.

said, "What is it honey?" *"I want to get a divorce."*

I remember thinking, "She's going to fall back in her chair and go, 'What?' " Mom did the exact opposite. She took my hands and said, "Honey I'm so sorry, but if that's what you want, then we'll be there." She was so supportive of my decision! Maybe she knew the marriage had been wrong from the start and had never said anything to me. She was so loving and caring, and more than anything, that's what I needed at that moment. I just needed validation—whether it was wrong or right—and mom definitely gave me that.

I knew my parents probably wouldn't like it, but mom was definitely there for me, regardless. I felt very much like her biological child at that moment. Mom really cared about me. "Is there any way it can be resolved?" she asked. *"No, mom."* "Okay," she said, "Then I'm behind you. We love you, honey, and we support you." These were very powerful words. Layers of fear and guilt began to melt away.

As a parent, if Luke were to tell me years from now, "Mom...I'm getting a divorce," I'd want so badly to encourage him to work it out. I'd probably advise counseling, or a marriage seminar...but really, I've learned the most important thing he'd need to know is that Larry and I love him and would be there for him *no matter what*. Mom did that extremely well for me. I had difficult days ahead, but I knew I wasn't alone.

Closing A Chapter of My Life

Keith was a wonderful person, but our marriage had been doomed to failure from the beginning. I hadn't married for the right reasons. I moved forward with the divorce in 1983, handling all of the legal matters myself. If there's one thing I did learn through this experience, it was that I should only marry for love—because marriage is a lifelong commitment.

I'm so thankful to God that I've met and married the love of my life. By His grace, marriage finally turned out well for me. And from what I understand, Keith is also doing well. He's married again and has two or three children. It's interesting to see how everything worked out.

As for the affair, it was over almost as fast as it began, but it was quite a learning experience. There was a lot of guilt associated with it; *after all, I'd grown up in church.* I had values and morals, but I didn't have a personal relationship with the Lord. So that was a definite challenge, especially until the divorce became final. After that, I was able to put it behind me. I regained strength and confidence, and turned to a new chapter of my life.

Unfortunately, I continued in a pattern of unhealthy romantic relationships. And I actually started repeating the same mistake—having affairs—only I wasn't the married party. I guess it somehow seemed okay for me to be involved with a married man, as long as I wasn't married. That's how stupid I was! Women hurt people every day doing this. Women like me. I wasn't concerned that my actions could potentially destroy the sanctity of a marriage. It didn't even occur to me! That's sad. I was self-centered, just looking out for myself.

I'd think, "This guy's coming on to me...and I'm attracted to him. If he has a problem in his marriage, that's *his* problem...I'm single. I'm not doing anything wrong." That's honestly how I felt! Many years later, however, I realized that I'd done everything wrong. How could I have even been an accomplice in a situation like that? What was I thinking?

> *I'm so thankful to God that I've met and married the love of my life. By His grace, marriage finally turned out well for me.*

Men are particularly vulnerable to women who act just like I did—who would do anything to get someone's attention. And like I said before, most affairs happen in the office, because that's where people spend most of their time, next to home. We must be wise; admit these situations can make us vulnerable. Larry and I, for example, always keep this is mind. When he's walking out the door, looking good, wearing my favorite cologne, I'll say something funny like, "You smell good today...got a date? Don't go out and have an affair..." We can joke about things like this, because we make an effort to keep the lines of communication open. This stamps out vulnerability.

Larry follows a principle that I think all men (and women) would do well to emulate. He never puts himself in a situation that's going to get him into a predicament where he can be tempted—because the devil loves to toy with your appetites. He knows he can get you that way! For instance, if Larry has a business lunch coming up and it includes a lady, he always tries to get another man from the business to go with him. If he can't find someone (or even sometimes if he does), he'll call me and say, "Barb, are you available for lunch? Can you come meet us?"

I have nothing to do with the business deal, but Larry invites me to demonstrate accountability to our relationship. It's like he's saying to me, "Barb, I'm putting you in this situation...not that I don't totally trust myself, but out of respect to you..." I love this about him. And I think if more people practiced this, a lot of affairs just wouldn't happen.

If you're married and have experienced a situation like I did at work, first of all, you need to let it rest and communicate with your husband. Decide together what you're going to do to show respect for one another, and then stop putting yourself in those situations. If you're single, think about the bigger picture and avoid these encounters altogether. From my experience, the temptation is you feel like a different breed...like this kind of relationship is justifiable because you're not married. *Don't buy into this deception.* Don't live according to the lust of the moment. Make yourself accountable. One of the best ways to start is by asking Jesus Christ into your life.

My "self-discovery phase" was actually more like a self-destruct cycle. And it lasted for many years...until I met and married Larry. I was preoccupied with myself...thought I was really something. If I hurt someone, I'd simply dust myself off, keep going, and rationalize, "That's okay, I'll just try to do better." For eleven, long years, I had that selfish, self-centered, attitude. "Look at me, I'm something. I'm going to make it. I don't care who I trample on to get there." I didn't realize I was doing the very thing that had wounded me as a child—*looking out for number one.* And whenever something better came along, I'd go for it.

Life is all about our experiences, and I still had a long way to go.

I'm eternally thankful to God for His love and mercy. God wants our relationships to be healthy and our marriages to succeed. Now I tell people, "If there's any glimmer of hope, you need to do whatever's necessary to make the marriage work." So if you're reading my story and you married for all the wrong reasons, first of all, *go to God.* Give Him your heart and ask for His wisdom and help. He loves you and will forgive your sins. He can bring good out of every situation. And remember, where there's an exit, you can always go around to the other side and find an entrance. With God, there's always hope for a better tomorrow...no matter what you're going through today.

> *Now I tell people, "If there's any glimmer of hope, you need to do whatever's necessary to make the marriage work."*

> *With God, there's always hope for a better tomorrow...no matter what you're going through today.*

Reflections

1. If you've ever had an affair, or know someone who has, did you or they come clean? Was the marriage salvaged? How tough has it been?

2. If you're single and have had an affair, did you consider the pain you were bringing to another person or family? What ultimately brought about feelings of conviction, or regret?

3. What do you think of the statement, "Where there's no accountability, there's no change in the behavior"?

Chapter 9

Houston, We Have A Problem
When Love Is Lost: Starting Over Again

After the divorce, I was still staying at our house and could barely afford to live there. Neither Keith nor I had hardly any money; he managed an electrical store and I was still working at the bank. And since there was no alimony in the State of Texas, and we didn't have any children, we just split everything up and went our separate ways.

I found myself in a quandary—there was definitely a problem. I was still very much in this self-discovery (destruct) mode—but where was Prince Charming? No matter whom I dated, I just couldn't find him. On top of that, since I hadn't gone to college, I was stuck making a minimal income. So I got a part-time job as a cocktail waitress at Steak & Ale (cocktailing was better money than waitressing) to supplement my income. That's how I was able to support myself.

It seemed life had taken a huge jump backwards. However, something amazing had happened during the early part of my marriage that indirectly helped me to keep my resolve. Even after my marriage had ended, this milestone event helped me come to terms with many layers of unresolved issues in my life. It helped me to get back on course. It was the entryway to my future after I'd left my past behind.

The Unexpected Call

About six months after Keith and I were married, I answered the phone one day and the voice on the other end said, "Barbara, do you know who this is?" *I knew.* I hadn't spoken with this person for a long time...since I was three years old. Up to that point, I knew of her—but never dreamed that she'd contact me. And I'd really formed no opinion of her, because my parents had been so good to not sway my opinion one way or the other.

It was my biological mother. She said, "Are you sitting down?" I was frozen, "No, but I can." "You do know who this is..." she continued. "Yes I do." "It's Carol, your mother...Honey, I'm so sorry to call you like this. Did you get my letter?" I hadn't received a letter; I didn't know what she was talking about. "The letter was to cushion this phone call...you didn't receive it?" I replied, "No, I didn't." Her first words after this were, "Do you hate me?"

It didn't take long for me to respond. "I don't hate you because I don't know you. How can I hate somebody that I don't know?" And she sighed, "Oh, good." I could tell she was getting a little choked up on the other end. It was so strange talking to this person who had given birth to me, *knowing of her* but not *knowing her.* I'd had another family my whole life, and hadn't had the desire to find her. I didn't know what to say. I just felt indifferent. I had no opinion either way.

To my surprise, we had an enjoyable conversation. As we caught up on the past eighteen years, I remember thinking that I liked her voice. And the whole time we were talking, I kept wondering what she looked like. I'd seen a few pictures of her when I was younger (we didn't have many around the house)—so I was extremely curious.

> *I answered the phone one day and the voice on the other end said, "Barbara, do you know who this is?" I knew.*

Chapter 9 / Houston, We Have A Problem

Unfolding The Mysteries of My Past

Dad and I hadn't talked about my biological mother, and mom hadn't said too much either—but I found out later that she definitely didn't have good feelings for Carol. And I discovered at some point after our first conversation that Carol had tried to contact me when I was younger.

Carol's first attempt turned out to be an horrific experience for my father. I was about four years old (approximately a year after she'd left us). Carol knew we were still living in Chicago and apparently had our address. She also knew my schedule. Basically, she kidnapped me. Carol knew that I'd be playing outside with other kids at a certain time, because we all lived in an apartment complex. So she and some people (I'm not sure who they were, and dad's never made it clear) picked me up and took me to the airport.

Dad was at work when it happened. I was being taken care of by the babysitter, but everything took place so quickly, there was nothing she could do. They just came and literally stole me from the play yard. She then flew me to her parents' house in Detroit, Michigan and left me with them, saying, "Don't tell John she's here." I lived with my grandparents for the next year and a half, until my father could work out custody.

At the time, I didn't know my grandparents very well (though we became close later). Upon arrival at their home, they immediately called my dad and said, "Your daughter's here." By this time, he was frantic. The babysitter had called him at work not knowing where I was, and in a panic, he'd immediately left the office. My grandparents cared deeply for my dad and me, and I think they knew their daughter was kind-of a loser at that point. It had to be very difficult for them.

As it turned out, my grandparents had adopted Carol and her sister when both girls were very young. Granddad had done well for himself as an OB/GYN. They had a fabulous three-story home with a basement, maids, a beautiful Labrador named Riley, and all the extras. Anyway, from that time forward, we developed a close relationship. Ultimately, dad sent me on vacation with them almost every year. We'd go to their summer cottage on Lake Superior and they'd treat me like a Princess.

After the kidnapping incident, the custody battles started. From what I understand, there was a lengthy litigation process, and afterwards, my dad was awarded custody (which was highly unusual in the early sixties). Women usually got custody of their children, but not in my case.

Carol's second contact came when I was about seven or eight years old (dad and mom were married by then and we were living in California). Carol called and said, "I want to speak with Barbara." I guess after everything they'd experienced, mom replied, "No, I don't want you talking to her. This isn't a good time. Don't call this house again." As a mother, I know mom was only doing what she thought was best. She didn't want anything hurting her family, and I can understand that.

Neither my parents nor Carol's family mentioned her during my childhood years. It was like nobody really knew how to talk about her. They didn't know how to act, or what to say. In the end, I realized they were all just trying to protect me.

My First Meeting with Carol

During our conversation, Carol and I agreed to meet each other within a couple of months. At

Chapter 9 / Houston, We Have A Problem

the time, she lived in California and Keith and I lived in Texas. She was planning to visit her father in Michigan and asked, "Wouldn't it be nice if we could meet in Detroit to visit your grandfather?" I agreed. It was an amazing visit. (Upon reflection, it reminds me of the talk shows I've seen where long lost relatives were reunited. It's a very uncommon experience...strangely unique, to say the least). During the flight, my mind kept churning..."What will she look like? Will I know who she is?"

Carol and I had told each other what we'd be wearing. My plane arrived earlier than hers, so I had about an hour or so wait upon landing. When her flight arrived, I just sat there and watched as people began filing off the plane. Then I stood up and watched closely, thinking as every woman came out, "Is that her?" *The moment she emerged, I knew.* I could have picked her out in the biggest crowd. She looked just like me, but older!

There we were. I was twenty-one and she was about forty-one. (I'm around that age now, which makes it somewhat of a sentimental time in my life. I can't help thinking if I had a daughter and were meeting her now...what would I do?) Anyway, I knew Carol right off the bat and she knew me. I remember her saying, "I saw you and I knew..." It was so incredible. We embraced, right there...talked, laughed...we just seemed to hit it off.

She kept telling me how beautiful I was, and that she was so proud of me. At that point in my life, I was starving for validation, drinking it up wherever I could—so hearing Carol say these wonderful things really helped me. It turned out to be quite a nice visit.

My grandmother had passed away two years before, but I enjoyed seeing my grandfather. They'd sold the home and he was living in a nursing home, so Carol and I went to see him

The moment she emerged, I knew. I could have picked her out in the biggest crowd. She looked just like me, but older!

I remember her saying, "I saw you and I knew..." It was so incredible. We embraced, right there...talked, laughed...we just seemed to hit it off.

127

there and spent time together. It was a little strange, though. She was affectionate toward him, but I could tell they hadn't been close. He was getting ready to go home and be with the Lord, and she was trying her hardest. Reflecting back, I think she'd tried to be a loving person her whole life, but it just didn't work for her.

The two weeks we were together, Carol never mentioned the kidnapping incident. (I didn't learn about it until later.) The only thing she was able to say during our time together was, "Do you hate me?" Carol was filled with guilt. She was really hurting inside and needed reassurance. So I assured her, "No, I don't hate you—but I'd like to get to know you..."

From then on, we continued building our relationship. I'd ask a few questions every now and then, and she'd answer them...but it took a process that spanned more than ten years. Finally, Carol confided that she just didn't want to be a mom. She wasn't ready. She had other priorities and things going on in her life, but she was profoundly sorry for what she'd done.

Carol also told me that she loved my father dearly, but was consumed with anger and rage (from things that happened in her past). She said, "Your father never laid a hand on me, but sometimes I had bruises from head to toe. I'd throw myself into him, almost beating him up. I wanted to fight, and I'd hurt myself just trying to get your father to fight back." Finally, I knew where my bad temper came from. Fighting was the way Carol dealt with things, but my father is such a gentleman. I believed her when she told me that he never laid a hand on her.

Years after our first meeting (when I worked for Southwest Airlines and could fly for free), I took regular trips to California where she lived with her family. Carol had been married a number of years when we met and had a twelve year old daughter named Erin. Over time, I built relationships with all of them.

It was difficult to imagine the pain and guilt my biological mother had to live with all of those years. She went on to tell me later that she'd written letters trying to make contact, but again, people kept shutting her off. Deep down, she knew she'd caused it.

Meeting Carol also gave me a better understanding of and appreciation for my parents. They'd done their best for me in a difficult situation. When Jan first met dad and me, she was living upstairs in the same apartment complex. And she saw this newly single man with an abandoned little girl. It must have touched her heart. As I grew up in our family, mom and dad did their best to help me overcome the pain of the past. I love them dearly for it.

> *Meeting my biological mother helped to heal a void in my soul....I could start over again and build a better future.*

Meeting my biological mother helped to heal a void in my soul. As I look back, I think it probably helped me to deal with my own mistakes in marriage. It gave me perspective. I knew though I'd made painful mistakes, I could start over again and build a better future.

Headed Back To College

So here I was: It was around 1985, and I was a 25-year-old divorcee. I was exhausted from working two jobs that paid very little. I was still into men, however, so somehow I always managed to fit in time for dating (I had to find my Prince Charming). I was going through guys like a box of chocolates.

The whole time, I remember thinking, "I messed up. I should have gone to college, because I could get a better job if I had a college education." This turned out to be a milestone in my life. I suddenly realized, "I can go to college!" Before, I didn't think it was possible. Now, my self-indulgent attitude was actually starting to become productive! I believed I could do anything I wanted to do. If I needed to go to college, so be it!

I started researching different institutions, finding out exactly what I had to do, what I could afford, where I could get loans, and so on. That's when I had an interesting conversation with my younger sister, Valorie. She was already a freshman at Tarleton State University in Stephenville, Texas.

I'd moved away from home several years before, and my family had moved to a little town called Springtown (about thirty miles northwest of Fort Worth). So unlike me, Valorie and Teresa had grown up in the country and attended a small, 2A level school. They were country girls! TSU was an agricultural school and part of the Texas A&M University system. It was a natural choice for small town people, kind-of a suitcase school. Students could attend during the week and go home on the weekends.

That gave me a great idea. So I said to Val, "You know what, maybe I'll join you and we can room together!" She was a little concerned, "Do you think you can do that, Barb?" "Yeah, I think I can. I can sell my stuff, move home to Springtown, and save enough money to get started...*whatever it takes*. I just need to ask mom and dad if I can live with them for six months. Then in the fall of '86, we'll go to school together!" She liked the idea.

And that's what I did. It wasn't easy, but I sold my house (sent half of the money to Keith), and moved back home with my parents. It seemed my life took another jump backwards. This time, however, I knew it was for the higher goal of finally going to college. Right away, I got a job working for an attorney whom I'd met at the bank (he liked me, of course, and offered

It seemed my life took another jump backwards. This time, however, I knew it was for the higher goal of finally going to college.

me a job as a legal secretary). He and his partner had a small firm in Arlington, almost two hours (one way) from Springtown. Thank goodness I was living at home with no expenses! I worked there for exactly six months.

A New Season Begins

I remember my first day on campus in 1986. Val and I decided to get an apartment, instead of living in the dorms (like she had during her freshman year). She was now a sophomore, and I was just getting started. At six years her senior, it felt a little weird! Anyway, we found a huge apartment right across the street from the campus for around $276 per month—that was next to nothing! It had two bedrooms (on opposite sides of the apartment), two full baths, an extra large living room, and a kitchen. It was wonderful. We lived there the entire time we were attending TSU.

Most of the students were just out of high school (the way it should be), mom and dad paying for their college expenses. For me, it was different. Although our parents were happy that I'd decided to go to college, and would have loved to pay for my college expenses, they'd already used the money they'd saved for my education. And it was impossible for them to cover expenses for both Val and me. I understood wholeheartedly; so I got loans for tuition and then got a job working the night shift at K-Bob's Family Restaurant to take care of living expenses. I knew that salary and tips would bring in more money.

I had a lot of young friends; many of them had no idea I was twenty-six. They told me they thought I was twenty-two or so. That made me feel good. Still, at times I felt old enough to be their grandmother—I guess it was what I'd already gone through in my life. My friends were really great, though. They always made me feel a part.

I also kept myself looking and feeling good by discovering a new sport: *bicycling*. While in college, I bought a bike for $75 and ended up entering a 30-mile race during my junior year. To my amazement, I won second place! I got $75 and a medal...*my bike had paid for itself.* When I got back home, I thought, "This cycling thing is fun..." so I started backing off from running. Cycling was much better on my legs and knees—less impact—and it was good for me. Besides that, I could eat as much as I wanted, because it really kept me in great shape.

Activities and friendships aside, I was fully committed to finishing my education. I told myself, "I'm going to get this degree and walk out of here. I shouldn't be here anyway." I earned my undergraduate degree in three years taking twenty-one hours a semester—with an almost full-time job! I worked three nights a week and all weekend from Friday to Sunday. Amazingly, I made the best grades of my life in college. I graduated in 1989 with a Bachelor of Business Administration degree in Finance...*with honors.*

> *I was fully committed to finishing my education.... I graduated in 1989 with a Bachelor of Business Administration degree in Finance...with honors.*

Let The Good Times Roll...

I definitely worked hard at my studies; however, Val and I always took time for play. Every now and then, we'd throw parties at our apartment— we really made it fun—but one night in particular, we made "trash can punch." What a night! We mixed Hawaiian Punch with about three bottles each of at least seven different kinds of liquor in a big, outdoor trash can. That thing was three-quarters full! We invited some friends, but by the end of the evening everybody from TSU was at our apartment...the word had gotten out about this punch!

We still get a lot of laughs whenever we remember that night. We tease each other, saying, "We really know how to throw a party!" It truly bonded us. As a matter of fact, Val and I became much closer during our college years. And we graduated around the same time; she finished about a semester before I did.

What's interesting, though, is the party ethic seemed to come with me when I left TSU. Little did I know, there would be much more to come.

A Romantic Twist

I didn't have a whole lot of time for dating in college. I did manage to fit it in, though, as usual. In fact, I'd just met someone before leaving for college that I liked a lot. He was still living with his parents and managed a restaurant in Arlington (where he lived). We always had a good time together. He'd either come to see me, or I'd go to Arlington and stay with him at his parents' house. We dated the whole time I was in college...but before it was over, he delivered the most devastating blow to me and my "I'm the greatest!" attitude.

One day (about a month before graduation), Daryl came to see me for the weekend and I went down to meet him in the parking lot. He got out of his car, opened his trunk, and said, "I've got a few things I need to give to you..." He took out a couple of books, a pillow, and some things I'd left at his house in Arlington. Then he said, "I'm leaving. I've been seeing this other girl for about a year. We're done."

I was shocked! "How dare you!" I thought. I'd cared about him, let my defenses down...and he abandoned me. It hit me like a brick. He was so cruel. He shut the trunk, got in the car, and drove off. I remember watching the back of

I'd just met someone before leaving for college that I liked a lot....but before it was over, he delivered the most devastating blow to me and my "I'm the greatest!" attitude.

his cool, sporty-looking little Nissan, thinking, "Unbelievable." Tears started streaming down my face. Stunned, I turned and started taking the long walk back to my building, sobbing the whole way.

After what seemed like an eternity, I reached the stairs. I remember staring at each step as I walked up, thinking, "Just let me get to the top..." I was incensed. "How could he do that to me?" I wondered. About half way up the stairs, I was crying so hard I started to hyperventilate. I literally couldn't breathe.

Finally, I got into my apartment and decided to call a friend who worked with me at K-Bob's. She lived in an apartment right across the street—so I dialed, "God, I hope she's there," I thought, "Because if she's not there, I don't know what I'll do." Thank goodness, Lynn was at home. "Come over and we'll talk," she said. I was beside myself; memories were flooding into my mind like crazy. There's no telling what I would have done, because I was in bad shape. I just knew somebody needed to help me.

After Lynn and I talked, I felt much better. Then I realized, "This guy's nothing." The real issue was, it was the first time a man had ever hurt me. That's why the pain went so deep. Prince Charming got another strike.

It was about two weeks before finals, which in turn, was two weeks before graduation. My schedule was overwhelming. I thought, "How could he do this to me...especially at test time?" I was over him in a week. And looking back, *who needed him?* More than anything, I'd hung onto our relationship because it made me feel secure. I could always count on Daryl when I needed something to do with my time.

Truth is, I fooled around with everybody in college that I could get my hands on! And I had the nerve to be upset when my "steady" boyfriend left me for someone else. I was crazy

How different would life have been if I had known the Lord?

It was the first time a man had ever hurt me. That's why the pain went so deep. Prince Charming got another strike.

to think, "You rat!" when I'd seen at least three or four guys pretty regularly during the course of our relationship! Talk about the pot calling the kettle black! It was okay for me to cheat on him, but not okay the other way around.

I'd come a long way in my education, but still had a lot to learn when it came to romance. My problems with men continued well into my career. Self-discovery was still very much a work in progress.

I'd come a long way in my education, but still had a lot to learn when it came to romance.

Reflections

1. Meeting my biological mother helped to heal my soul. Have you had a turning point in your life where a hole in your heart was filled? What was it and how did it help you?

2. Have you ever felt like you've done things backwards in life? Maybe against the norm? How did you deal with it?

3. Think about a time when you were hurt severely by someone. Did you think you just couldn't make it? What brought you through?

4. How different would my reaction have been if I'd known the Lord when Daryl left me? (Remember, my abandonment issue was very intense, even after I'd met my biological mother.) How do you think people who don't know the Lord get through these types of situations?

Chapter 10

Living The High Life
Self Love: The Hardest Lesson

When I graduated from college, I didn't have a clue what I was going to do. I did know, however, I was ready to leave Stephenville and start a new, exciting life. I remember telling the girls I worked with at K-Bob's, "When I graduate, you're going to see my little brown Mazda GLC zip down Main Street and get out of town so fast..." I'd worked hard, finished college faster than usual, closed down my apartment—*and I felt great.* Then it hit me, "Now what do I do?"

I knew I had to get to work, but I didn't know how to go about it: So I turned my car around and went back, and then reopened my apartment. I wanted to work in Dallas, but thought, "I'll have to look for jobs from here. I need a place to job hunt." So I bought some index cards and set up an office in my apartment. Val had already taken most of the furniture, so I sat in my big, scarcely furnished home base and started the hunt.

I got the paper every day and scanned the job listings. Finally, I was able to arrange interviews at some companies in Las Colinas (a western suburb of Dallas), and about two months after that, landed an interview with Southwest Airlines.

The Thrill of Independence

I'd never thought about working for an airline company, but considered giving it a try. At the same time, I was struggling with whether or not I really wanted to get a job as a financial analyst. So I kept thinking to myself, "You know Barb, *you do* want to be a financial analyst. That's what you earned a degree to do...yes, it's your personality—to sit behind a desk and be an analyst." I kept convincing myself this is what I really wanted. Not a good sign.

At the time, Southwest was starting a new department they referred to as Revenue Management. They were going to pick five people out of approximately five hundred applications. So I went through a series of interviews, thinking I didn't have a chance, and they hired me! I thought, "I'm a Revenue Financial Analyst. Okay! Here I go!" I was entering the high life at one of the nation's most highly acclaimed organizations.

It wasn't long after I started working at Southwest that I bought my first car. I'd seen a television commercial about "The New Mitsubishi Eclipse" years before while preparing to go to college. This was a brand new model! No one had ever heard of it before; so when I saw the ad I said, "That's what I'm going to have someday..." Sure enough, within a year after graduating I bought a brand new Mitsubishi Eclipse. This definitely was a milestone. I was driving to work in style.

We underwent intensive training for the new department and computer system. The finance job was fun and exciting. I'd sit in my little cubicle, analyze seats on flights, and get the most money possible for every one of them. I'd take seats away and put seats out, constantly watching the demand of the market. I could watch flights up to six months in advance, seeing how people were booking them.

It was simple economics, supply and demand. If a flight was popular (maybe there was going to be a convention in town), then I'd stop selling the cheap seats and make the more expensive ones available...because the demand was there. People were going to buy a ticket, regardless. Of course, I performed other duties, but that was my primary function during my first three years with the company.

The only problem was I started drinking more and more, to the point of abuse. It was worse than at any other time in my life, and it intensified as I pursued my career.

Going After The Career of My Dreams

I liked my job, but I couldn't help thinking, "I have much more personality than this; I could be doing something else." At the time, Southwest had 17,000 employees, and one day I noticed the company had a department called the University for People. (Southwest was very personable. What most companies call Human Resources, they refer to as The People Department...) I thought, "Wow, it would be really cool to work there. I wonder what they do?" I liked the name, so I started looking into it.

There were a vast array of things to do at the University, but there were only four instructor's positions (which were all filled). The trainers were top notch: two male and two female. These were high profile positions, because every employee had to take classes—and most of them were mandatory.

Instructors interacted with literally thousands of people in the company, from Mail Clerks to Flight Attendants, all the way up to the Chief Executive Officer. If someone got promoted to a supervisory or management position, or he wanted to take a course in time or stress management—he'd enroll for classes. I thought, "Boy, it would be the greatest thing to be an instructor there."

Normally, there wasn't much movement in the instructor's positions. Whoever held a position usually kept it for quite some time. Then suddenly, with the company's rapid growth, people started moving and new positions became available. Over the course of a year and a half, I applied four times and got turned down. The second year of my pursuit (sometime around 1992), a fifth position opened up.

As part of the interview process, applicants were required to develop and present a pilot program. And, of course, there was the one-on-one interview. (Actually, there were a series of four or five interviews, all with different requirements.) Each time I applied, I went through this same, long sequence of events.

I could have gotten through this arduous process so much better if I had God in my life—especially after having been turned down four times. I felt like the biggest failure, but I just knew I could do this job! It wasn't in the area of my degree...but I could do it! It fit my personality.

If I had God in my life, I would have known it was all about timing. Everything happens in God's timing, not ours. I would have been secure in the fact that God knows best—not me.

A Winning Presentation

By then, I was depressed and drinking a lot. Drinking had become my way of escape; I felt like such a loser. I never gave up, but I definitely wasn't coping properly. I kept thinking, "I can do this thing." This time, I called a friend to help me, "Bill, you have to help me with this presentation. I have to get this job..." He was glad to help. We went to a bar and literally closed it down that night writing a program for my next interview (two days later).

Two beers into the evening, he said, "Okay, let's write it down on a napkin." So there we were, getting drunk and writing a new program on a skimpy piece of paper. It was actually pretty creative. We came up with a Vegas Casino-type presentation, making our topic applicable to life using the game of Black Jack.

The more we drank, the wilder the ideas became. I remember Bill saying something like, "Yeah, Barb, you could even do a magic trick with the cards!" He took out his deck of cards and did this magic trick for me. "Oh, that's so amazing!" I exclaimed. (It sounds stupid now, but while we were getting inebriated, it seemed like the coolest thing!)

Another reason I had this "anything goes" mentality was that I was fed up...I'd had it! I'd been turned down for my dream position four times. I had nothing to lose, so I went for it! After I sobered up, I fine-tuned the presentation and it was fantastic! I presented it during the interview and even did something with playing cards as part of the program. They loved it. I got the job!

Immediately, I called Bill, "I got it! Come celebrate with me!" We went out and closed down the bar again, celebrating something we'd created while under the influence. This reminds me of a story I heard recently about the renowned author, Stephen King. In one of his books, he apparently said he couldn't remember how he wrote his blockbuster hit, *Cujo!*[1] Imagine doing your best work in an "altered" state of mind. I actually thought, "Hey, that drinking really helps..." This sent me headlong into an even more destructive drinking habit.

I believe the real dynamic that yielded this winning presentation was teamwork. Up to that point, I'd been trying to do everything myself. When I'd gone past the point of no return, I enlisted my friend's help, thinking: "Maybe two minds can get this thing rolling." That's where the power was, not in the fact that we were drinking! If you're up against a wall, don't ever make the mistake of thinking you have to come

If I had God in my life, I would have seen that alcohol wasn't going to help my career. Instead, it would hinder my work and my quality of life.

up with the solution alone. When good minds come together, you can brainstorm and come up with things you've never imagined.

Many times, we want to do things alone so we can say, "Look what I did!" That way, we're privy to the information. We don't want to share the glory with anybody. That's how I was for so many years: I had to be the only one to come up with all the answers. However, when I thought I had nothing to lose, I pulled somebody else in just to see what happened. That was my first realization of teamwork...but the alcohol hindered my perception. By working together, Bill and I came up with something much stronger than I could have done on my own.

The Real Partying Begins

I enjoyed being a Corporate Trainer, and was quite good at it. It was a big time in my life. I was meeting all the right people, and flying anywhere I wanted to go for free. I started partying hard and drinking heavily; this lasted from 1992 through 1994 (when I met Larry). I thought I was on top of the world, but in reality, I was creating new layers of iniquity that would have to be dealt with later.

Incredibly, I wasn't curtailed from my other physical activities. I was entering cycling races all over Dallas and Fort Worth, and won two more medals. I was fascinated with sports and tried as many as I could: water-skiing, snow skiing, hiking, golf...*you name it,* I was trying it and loving it. Sports even became a part of my new duties as a trainer when I started teaching Ropes Courses (kind of an Outward Bound experience for employees). The whole idea was to send each participant through an outdoor experience that made them reach new limits, see new potential in themselves, and build trust in others. Basically, it was a confidence building exercise—and it was very effective.

We'd go to an area outdoors that had been set up with apparatuses called "low elements" and "high elements" (like rock climbing walls, and so on). One of the high elements was a 30-foot telephone pole that participants were told to climb, balance on top, and then jump off into a trampoline. (Don't panic, though, they were supported by all kinds of ropes and hardware. Participants were actually quite safe.) I'd see people get down to the bottom of that element and literally weep...*because they'd been transformed.* They'd done something they never thought they'd be able to do.

My job was to make each experience applicable to their lives and work. I'd ask questions like, "What limits have you placed on yourself that you know don't need to be there, because of what you were just able to do?" or "How can you work better as a team?" I became adept at climbing walls and doing all sorts of challenging physical activities.

During this time, however, I only got small promotions. They just weren't what I wanted, as quickly as I thought they should have come. Ultimately, I wanted to become the department manager—but I could never get there. Alcohol was keeping me up late at night, and it was becoming increasingly difficult to concentrate on my work. I'm sure my lifestyle had a lot to do with it. I was tired. As much as I enjoyed my work, I couldn't have been giving it my best efforts.

All the while, I was disappointing myself. It was a familiar pattern. I'd wake up from a stupor and think, "I'll do better tomorrow," or "I'll do better this weekend."

My conscience couldn't handle doing these same things today. I'd be hurting my heavenly Father so deeply that I couldn't bear it! I'm so

If I had God in my life, I would have been accountable to Him. I would have realized that I wasn't disappointing myself alone, but also my heavenly Father. That would have kept me on a much better track.

thankful that God is in my life. He gives me such awareness and accountability. I still have to deal with sin, like anyone else, but I'm a far cry from what I was before. Every now and then, I slip up—just like anybody else—but there's no way I could live in habitual sin.

For some reason, though, I thought I was really onto something in those days. I'd finished college and had a high profile position at Southwest. I was single, flying all over the country doing corporate training...*and partying.* I was trying to make it all work, and burning the candle on both ends.

Who Me? Gambling?

Sometime during this adventure, I discovered Las Vegas and started getting into gambling. Alcohol was the big thing in Vegas. They give you free drinks. So really, the alcohol got me to Vegas and the gambling just sort-of happened. When I found out that I could sit at a Black Jack table for hours with free drinks, *I was sold.* As long as you play in casinos, everything's free— because they want you to sit there and lose every dime you have.

I started gambling all my money away...and I didn't have much to gamble! Some think a gambling problem means losing hundreds of thousands of dollars. I didn't have anywhere near that amount to lose, but I definitely had an addiction. Before I knew it, I was going to Vegas every other weekend for at least a year.

I played Black Jack and Video Poker the most...and I really loved Video Poker—but the odds were best at Black Jack. I'd get bored with Jack, though, and go back to my first love (Poker). I'd take money with me to Vegas, and then when it ran out, I'd go to the automatic teller machine and debit my accounts. And when that didn't work anymore, I started taking cash advances off of my credit card.

My Final Wake Up Calls

Thank God, I finally woke up. I was standing at an ATM putting my credit card in the slot...shaking because I'd lost everything. I just knew if I had *one more chance*, I could win it back. I stopped and thought, "Ooh, you've got a real problem, Barb."

I still love Vegas, but I don't go there much because I know it can be tempting. It's really a beautiful city. It has all the things that are associated with success: *lights*, *glamour*, *entertainment*, and *fun*. Las Vegas is a great tourist attraction...but when I think about what it's done to people, how they've probably lost everything they have—it hurts me. It's hard to think about that. I turned over this area of my life to God. Now, He's in control. And I'm extremely aware.

Anyway, I was tired of drinking and partying. I was in my early thirties, and had come to the point where I just couldn't take it anymore. I was abusing myself. My throat was raw from smoking so many cigarettes. I thought, "I have to quit this!" I was getting concerned for my health, afraid of what would happen if I didn't stop. I was tired of the whole scene...in short, I woke up. I wasn't performing at work. I was so tired every morning, I thought, "I have to stop...*I have to stop.*" I was really trying to get promoted, and it wasn't happening. I wanted more money. I'd think, "Gosh I have to get promoted. I know I have it in me. What's keeping me from it?"

Drinking and late night runs to Vegas, New Orleans (and other places) were taking their toll on me. According to Southwest's policy, you could fly any of their routes for free, if a seat was available on standby—but don't ever go somewhere and then not get home and report back to work. In other words, if you don't have your plans worked out and end up missing time at work, you've lost your job. Employees had to be very careful.

My position was so flexible, though, I could go to Vegas on Thursday and return on Saturday. If that didn't work, I could go Friday night and come back early Monday morning—when seats were more likely to be available. Friday and Sunday were the busiest flight days, so one could easily wait for hours on Friday night trying to get a flight. When that happened, I'd come back to Dallas on Monday morning totally exhausted.

When I partied in town, I'd drink like a sailor and then have to drive home. And since I was single, I might stop at some guy's house (I'd been partying with) first...but eventually, I'd come home—or he'd come with me. It's awful when I think of how I lived back then. I'd be driving home on a two-lane road, but I'd be seeing six lanes of lights.

There'd be three or four cars coming toward me on the other side of the highway, but I'd see dozens of lights. It looked like a football stadium. I didn't know which light to follow. I'd be wondering, "How many lanes are there?" Many times, I'd wake up the next day not knowing where my car was. I'd walk out of my apartment thinking, "Gosh, I hope my car is in the parking lot. I think I remember parking it..."

One night I had an accident. It wasn't serious; I was coming to a stop at a red light and hit the car in front of me. I was drunk, so I didn't judge the distance properly. Anyway, the car was torn up before I hit it, but a guy got out and started walking toward me. I looked at him and thought, "Oh, my gosh!" I was so drunk, I

Chapter 10 / Living The High Life

couldn't stand up—so I got in my car and left. He wasn't hurt, but I panicked.

Another night, I backed into a pole and knocked out my taillight (it was really late...after a Dallas Mavericks game, or some event of that magnitude). Paranoid, I thought somebody was going to see me and pull me over, so it took me three hours to get home. Every time I'd see a police car, I'd pull down a road I didn't know, or pull into people's driveways (cutting my lights)...trying to avoid them. It was awful.

One time, I came upon a bad accident. I was the first one there, and I was drunk. I stopped, ran over to the car and said, "Are you okay?" The woman said, "I think I'm okay." I ran back to my car thinking, "Barb, you can't get help. You're drunk!" So I sat in my car and waited until another car stopped, *and then I left.* I couldn't stick around to witness and give a report, because I was afraid they'd take me to jail.

A huge wake up call came one day as I was watching the news. There were so many frightening reports: a child had been run over in the street in one story, and there was another one about a hit and run. I couldn't help thinking, "What if I had done that?" Worse yet, I realized that I could do it! Then it hit me, "Barb, what if you have, and you don't even remember?" I thought I was lucky, but actually, God was protecting me...from myself.

> *I didn't know God yet, but I believe in all these things, He was with me—protecting me from myself.*

No More Disposable Relationships

Needless to say, during the majority of my time at Southwest, I didn't have any serious relationships. In fact, almost any relationship would do. When I traveled to Colorado or Utah, I'd meet guys that had cabins or ski lodges...and then call them in the winter saying, "Hey, what are you doing?" All through the

> *I didn't have any serious relationships. In fact, almost any relationship would do.*

winter months, I'd meet up with guys that had those things. I'd use them, take advantage of the ski resort amenities, and whatever else.

During summer, I'd find the guys that had sailboats, water skis, and those types of things, and hook up with them. I used to make it sound okay by saying to myself, "I'm dating now. I can date anybody I want." In some cases, I was being intimate with these men! That was wrong. I was willing to get men to like me, just to get all the stuff I wanted (trips, lodges, ski lessons, money, whatever). I wasn't a nice person. My values were all mixed up.

A final romantic experience shook me into reality. I'd been partying with a guy one night (around 1992–93) and ended up at his apartment afterwards. I'd worked with him, played sports with him—he was just a good buddy. And he was attractive. When we got to his apartment, he started getting fresh with me. I didn't mind, I kind of wanted him to, so we started getting fresh with each other. That's when the mood started to shift.

He started getting pretty forceful, and it scared me. So I said, "No, Sam, I don't want to do that..." He said, "Yeah, you do, and you know you do." He pushed me down so hard that I fell on the couch. Now, I was really afraid. I protested, "No, no...I'm telling you no! That's what I'm telling you." "But I don't hear your 'no,' " he snapped, "Every indication you've given me has been *yes*." Then he got on top of me and started getting pretty rough.

At this point, I was terrified. I thought, "This man's going to rape me." And I'd walked right into this situation! It was almost like he'd baited the trap and I just pranced right in. I remember thinking, "If I scream, it's going to make me look stupid, because this is the most awkward situation..." I shoved him back (and I remember him looking at me funny), and then I started screaming. I really thought this guy was going to go bezerk on me! I pushed him back and screamed, "No, absolutely not! Don't!" and ran toward the door. He tried to grab me and I screamed at him again.

I had to keep moving. Thank God, the door was unlocked, so I bolted outside and ran to the car in tears. And I was looking over my shoulder the whole time to see if he was coming after me; but he wasn't. He was just standing in the doorway. I got in my car and drove home in tears, thinking, "I was almost raped!" It was a terrifying moment. Even worse, I had to face him at work...and I never spoke to him again. We just went our separate ways.

Situations like this can happen all too easily, and sadly, they happen every day. It's called date rape. Goofing off with guys like I did was dangerous; because you never know what kind of situation you're going to walk into.

That was my moment of truth. I decided then to change my life. I just told myself, "You don't need to be doing this stuff," and stopped. I finally wanted to be in control, so I seized the opportunity. I made the choice that I didn't want to live like that anymore. Now I know it was God who gave me the strength to do it (even though I didn't realize it at the time). I knew I couldn't live that way any longer, or I was going to get into serious trouble. *I could feel it.* Something bad was going to happen if I didn't stop this cycle.

I realized that not only was I using men, they were using me! And I was abusing myself. *Voila!* What a revelation. So I decided, *"No more men. No more heavy drinking.* I'm not going to date anyone. I'm going to do some growing on my own." During the next year, I worked on cleaning up my act and becoming a better, more responsible person. My self-destructive cycle was finally over.

Goofing off with guys like I did was dangerous; because you never know what kind of situation you're going to walk into.

I made the choice that I didn't want to live like that anymore. Now I know it was God who gave me the strength to do it...

We change because it's too painful to stay where we are.

A lot of people have to get professional help for drinking problems and some of the other things I was dealing with. If that's the case, then so be it. People shouldn't be ashamed when they realize they need help to overcome a destructive habit. They should be happy and thankful they were smart enough to say, "This isn't how I want my life to be...*I need help.*" There's nothing wrong with checking into a rehabilitation center, or going to a counselor if that's what you need. On the other hand, there's a real problem with living in denial. *When you're able to admit you have a problem, it says a lot about you.*

An Interesting Turn in My Heart

So here I was, starting fresh in my early thirties. That's when I began to notice how many people were asking me why I wasn't married. I had a decent job, and it appeared to everyone that I was happy and had everything going for me. It seemed I was their perfect candidate for a serious relationship. Well, I got tired of all the questions. I actually started second-guessing myself, thinking, "Maybe there is something wrong with me, maybe I am holding out for a little too much. Maybe I'm not worth as much as I believe I am."

Then I came back to my senses. "No way!" I was confident that I could have a better life and still believed there was a special man out there for me. He would love me, and I would love him—*sincerely.* It happened when I met Larry. *I knew.* For Larry and me, I'd say it was probably love at first sight...I just didn't realize it until I was gripping the steering wheel on my way to the airport for a date with another man. Larry and I had only dated twice; yet no matter how hard I tried, I couldn't get him out of my mind.

Looking back, I know more than ever that God was with me—even before I received Jesus Christ into my heart. Now, I can recall all of the times He gently helped me find my way...until I'd reached the point where I could meet the love of my life. God had a wonderful future in store for me, and it was just around the corner.

'For I know the plans I have for you,' declares the LORD, 'plans to prosper you and not to harm you, plans to give you hope and a future. Then you will call upon me and come and pray to me, and I will listen to you. You will seek me and find me when you seek me with all your heart.'
Jer. 29:11–13, NIV

---

[1] King, Stephen. *On Writing: A Memoir of The Craft*, p. 99. Pocket Books, a division of Simon & Schuster, Inc., New York, NY. Copyright © 2000.

Reflections

1. It's been said that we change when it's too painful to stay where we are. Have you had moments like this? What were they? Did you take command of your life on your own, or did you seek help and/or guidance? Either way, I'd call that taking command of your circumstances and refusing to be a victim!

2. Is it apparent to you that we have choices in everything we think and do? We are where we are in life due to the choices and decisions we've made (or someone else has made for us). Remember, ten percent of life is what happens to us and ninety percent is how we respond to it.

3. Have you ever thought for a brief moment that your life could be in danger? What did you do? How have you changed because of that experience? What was the outcome? Can you look back now and see when God was protecting you in a difficult situation?

Chapter 11

Know It? I Wrote It.
Perfect Love: Resting in God

Not long ago, I thought if I was ever to get breast cancer, I wouldn't be discouraged. I'd just choose to look at the glass half full—a mastectomy could only mean implants, and I've always wanted to have larger breasts. So what could be so bad about it? *It terrifies me to admit that thought even crossed my mind.* How superficial could I be? Everybody knows that breast cancer goes much deeper than the mere appearance of a woman's breasts. Literally.

My point is, we tend to think only about the surface things—what people see, what looks good, and what's acceptable. We look for "things" to make us happy, like money, materialism, spouses, and success. Yet there's something deeper within us; it runs through our veins, fills our soul, and takes over our entire being. We are spiritual beings. *We need God.*

As I was thinking about a title for this chapter, I couldn't help reflecting on the goodness of God. He's taken care of every storm in my life—the early abandonment, relationship failures, and destructive habits—all the layers of sin and self that were standing in the way of my destiny. In everything, God has been faithful. So I shouldn't worry about things that are insignificant in view of eternity.

Father Knows Best

God knows it because He wrote it. So why bother worrying about a lump in my breast, a

> *Do not be anxious then, saying, 'What shall we eat?' or 'What shall we drink?' or 'With what shall we clothe ourselves?'....But seek first His kingdom and His righteousness; and all these things shall be added to you.*
> Matt. 6:31–33

> *And we know that God causes all things to work together for good to those who love God, to those who are called according to {His} purpose.*
> Rom. 8:28

career that's over, or the fact that our son may not be potty trained yet? God sees the end, and He's not worried. He's sitting on His throne in heaven thinking, "She's preoccupied with all these things that I'm working together for her good." The fight's already been fixed—in our favor—*but we don't see it.* It's like a crowd at a professional fight that's yelling like crazy because they don't know what's going to happen next. At the same time, the owners are really calm. The crowd's frantic because they don't know the fight's already been fixed. They don't know what the owners know.

Our heavenly Father created the universe. He's sitting back, the epitome of peace, saying, "You guys are something." He's looking at our lives saying, "You worry too much." That's why Philippians 4:6–7 says, "Don't worry about anything; instead, *pray about everything*; tell God your needs, and don't forget to thank him for his answers. If you do this, you will experience God's peace, which is far more wonderful than the human mind can understand. His peace will keep your thoughts and your hearts quiet and at rest as you trust in Christ Jesus" (TLB).

Forever in God's Care

Everything comes full circle. I remember when I was sixteen years old and got my first kiss...I dreamed about it afterwards! I waited my whole life to experience that magical moment again. Then I met Larry. And I'll always remember our wedding night. Larry and I had taken a boom box to Jamaica, along with a Platter's tape of those old love songs like *Only You* and *Smoke Gets In Your Eyes*. We danced and danced in our hotel suite...and as we moved, we heard the gentle clicking of our heels caressing the beautifully tiled floor. It was like a dream.

Larry actually created a cassette tape of five love songs and gave them to me on our fifth anniversary. I listened to the songs and started to cry, thinking how much time and effort it had taken him to produce it. The other night, we listened to the songs again. *Fairytales do come true, if you want them badly enough!* Our life hasn't always been a bed of roses; but it's definitely ending up that way. To think I was once afraid of what I'd have to give up after accepting Christ! I've gained more blessings than I could have ever imagined. Larry is my Prince Charming, and God is my King. Life couldn't be better.

Luke is about three years old. He wants to spend time with me, but I know it won't always be that way. One day, I'll be trying to find Luke for the same reason. This is such a precious time. The fact is, I'm raising my son, so I'm learning to be less busy. I'm trying to stop saying things like, "I have to wash the dishes, Luke, because your father's going to be home in an hour. Dinner has to be ready..." Does this really matter? Will my husband love me whether or not I have dinner on the table? Of course, he will! And my son will be a better man someday, because we spend quality time together *right now*.

And then there are Larry's two sons, Larry Glenn and Bobby. When we started dating, Larry Glenn had just graduated from high school and was thinking about going to college. He was still living with his dad in San Antonio and helping with the roofing company. Larry had dated several women before me, and Larry Glenn didn't like any of them.

One night after I'd returned to Dallas from one of our dates, Larry called me and said, "Larry Glenn wants to talk to you." I was surprised when he shared, "I think you're really good for my dad..." He was so complimentary!

Then Larry got back on the phone and said, "Let me tell you something. He's never said that to any woman I've dated." I've never forgotten what Larry Glenn said that night. It meant everything to me. And now he's been married almost five years...to a wonderful woman.

Bobby, on the other hand, was three years younger than Larry Glenn and lived with his mother. So after we were married, he spent summers and some holidays with us. Now he's twenty-four and married to someone special. I'm still remembering the day he got his first car...*wow!*

Both boys have always been so respectful to me, and I love them very much. I've also made sure to have pictures of their mother in our home, and Larry thinks it's terrific. I've been so blessed! I've done nothing to deserve the life we have. Many times when people with older children get married, the kids can become a problem. Larry's children were never that way. They've always been wonderful.

I can't ever say too much about my dad! He loved and protected me when his own life was falling apart. I was his little Cinderella, and he was my first Prince Charming. I remember when I was young and he'd visit my school on Parent's Day. I'd gaze at him and think, "Wow, he's so handsome! Would you look at my father! That's my father!" We laugh about it now, because he's a lot shorter (mostly because I've gotten taller!). I still tell him, though, "Dad, you were so handsome then, and you still are..." His love filled me with confidence.

I couldn't have asked for a better mom. Jan came into my life and literally changed my destiny. Where would I be without her? She's a priceless gift from God. People don't value stay-at-home moms nearly as much as they should—because these days, being at home is definitely not synonymous with care and nurturing! Mom is truly exceptional. She shaped me into the responsible, independent person I am today.

My parents and I haven't always stayed in regular contact; there were seasons when my life was so hectic, we lost touch. We usually managed to get together on holidays, though, and talked every now and then. Now, with all of the grandchildren, we're getting together more often—especially for birthdays.

Both Val and Teresa are doing well. Teresa ended up attending Texas Tech University in Lubbock and is still living there today. She and her husband have a son, Reagan, and own a business. They've done well for themselves. Val left TSU in Stephenville and got a job in Oklahoma City, Oklahoma. Now she's back in Texas and lives in a suburb of Dallas called Flower Mound. She's got a great position with TXU Energy and has two sons, Jordan and Matthew.

If you were to put our personalities in order of intensity, Teresa would be at the top. She's a fireball. Teresa's so much fun to be with! When she walks into a room, people gravitate to her. She's funny, loud, and smiles all the time. I'm in the middle (and I think you have a good idea what my temperament is like!). Val's kind of quiet and reserved. She's extremely careful about what she says, and always thinks things through completely before speaking. Val's very methodical; I love that about her. We formed a special bond in college. We both crack up whenever we remember the night we made "trash can punch." I'll joke with her and say, "Do you remember how good we were at having parties?" Now, we're planning our next family reunion. Scary thought, huh?

Our parents had three girls, but all the grandchildren have been boys! Now they're hoping for girls! Dad liked boys, so as a result, we all turned out to be tomboys. We just love telling him, "Now you have your boys, and you want girls...we don't get it! You wanted this, and this is what God has given you." He just laughs.

Dad's the greatest grandfather. He's so hands-on, and makes himself available whenever any of us needs him. If we give him enough advance notice (let's say a couple of days), he'll come in a second. And he's so good with the boys; he's actually a lot like a grandmother! He bathes them, changes diapers...*I just love seeing him in action.* When we were growing up, dad was so busy working that we rarely saw him. So mom stayed home and did a terrific job taking care of us. Now she has a job and her hours aren't so flexible. It's interesting. Mom used to be the nurturer and disciplinarian, and now (because dad's work schedule is more flexible) their roles have reversed.

Seeing the "nurturing" side of my dad truly amazes me! When he comes over he doesn't just say, "Okay kids, go play." He gets right down with them, whether it's playtime, bath time, or dinnertime. In fact, I could call him right now and say, "Dad, I've got a women's retreat coming up. I need you to take care of Luke for the entire weekend. Do you want me to bring him to your house [two hours away], or do you want to come to my house and keep him here (around his familiar surroundings)?" He'd say, "What's easier for you?" And he'd be available to do whatever worked best for me. No questions asked. He's just a great guy!

Larry's mother has had a profound influence on my life. And she's the most awesome grandmother! She's very hands-on with Luke: She wants to see everything he does and keeps up with his every move. I couldn't be more blessed! She's the ripe, young age of seventy-one and lives in Pine Bluff, Arkansas (Larry's hometown).

We see each other often. She visits with us maybe three or four times a year, and we visit her around twice a year. Larry and I feel totally comfortable going to her house and saying, "Here, have Luke." Then we just keep on going! We trust her completely. She's a real go-getter, and keeps herself in great shape. She gets around like she's forty!

On top of everything else, she's such a godly woman—always reading her Bible, attending church, and so on. She has a vital relationship with the Lord. It's like she's my spiritual mentor—I often catch myself repeating things I've heard her say. I'll bet she's witnessing my spiritual growth (since that first telephone call) and is thinking, "Wow." God's been so good.

God Is Faithful in All Things

My biological mother, Carol, did well in her second marriage. She and her husband were together until he died, which was about two years before she passed away in July 2000. They'd had a long marriage and a wonderful child. Erin is so beautiful. She's a single mom now and has two great kids; yet she managed to attend classes for three years and become a court reporter. She recently graduated and has started her own home business. I'm so proud of her.

Carol's passing saddened me. She'd suffered from chronic leukemia for ten years, so it became increasingly difficult for her from about 1990 to 2000. Often, she had to be hospitalized (because the effects of leukemia are similar to AIDS). It really broke down her immune system, making it difficult for her body to fight off even the simplest of colds. At times, the leukemia would go into remission and she'd start feeling a lot better, and then it would get worse again. We lived with that sickness.

Eventually, Carol and her husband moved to Texas. Erin had told her how nice it is in Dallas...how good the weather is, and so on. They'd lived in their house in California all of their married life, but sold it to start a new life in Texas. And Carol did get better. In fact, she went into remission for about four or five years. Then around 1999, the leukemia started progressing. From that point on, Carol was literally in and out, so I'd go and spend time with her and Erin at their home in McKinney.

Carol died while Larry and I were out of town. She did get to see Luke as a baby, though, and I was glad that she did. I believe she was saved and that she's in heaven now, because she attended our church a number of times. Church really hadn't been her thing (in the earlier years), but I think she came enough that she finally asked Jesus to come into her heart.

After the funeral, Erin and I picked up Carol's ashes. I'd never done anything like that before. We went to a funeral home and got this little box—and it was so heavy! When Erin picked it up, I said, "Let me feel it. It's weird...very strange." I couldn't believe how heavy it was. She then flew to California, got together with some old friends, and scattered Carol's ashes out over Catalina Bay.

Erin came back and put the empty box in a back room at her house, where Carol stayed while she was sick (so as not to infect the children). Erin didn't clean the room for a long time. Carol's death had affected her deeply. I was sad when Carol died, but knew my pain wasn't nearly as deep as Erin's. About six months later, though, I was sitting in the bathtub and thought about her. I realized she was really gone, and cried.

I'm not sure how long the grief process will last, but I know I loved her. Yes, Carol had made serious mistakes—we all do—*but she gave me life.* I'm so thankful. She was a good person, but had made some bad decisions, and ended up living with a lot more pain than I did...because I had my family. Still, I know Carol's in heaven.

Erin moved to Texas seven years ago and still lives in McKinney. We keep in contact. She attends church maybe once or twice a year; in fact, I saw her this past Easter. The night before, she called me and asked, "What time is the service?" "10:30." "Well, I'll be there." When she walked in, I said, "Oh, it's so good to see you!" She replied, "I'm just doing my good thing." I understand where she is, because I used to feel exactly the same way. I'm excited to see what God's going to do in her life.

Erin's a great person, and I'm trying to be a good aunt to her kids. Luke and I pray for them every night. In fact, we always pray for *everyone.* Luke has such a wonderful extended family. God's been so faithful to us.

I Choose Happiness

Everybody has problems. My life's a prime example—but I've also been tremendously blessed. So I've learned to stop and smell the roses. Ten o'clock this morning is already gone. There's nothing I can do to change it. I can change *this moment*, though. I can choose to make it exactly what I want it to be—*so I choose happiness!* I choose joy!

Now when I read Larry's note in my Bible, it almost scares me. It's as though he foreknew what God had in store for my life. I finally understand why Larry wrote, "This is the

---

Finally, brethren, whatever is true, whatever is honorable, whatever is right, whatever is pure, whatever is lovely, whatever is of good repute, if there is any excellence and if anything worthy of praise, let your mind dwell on these things. The things you have learned and received and heard and seen in me, practice these things; and the God of peace shall be with you.
Phil. 4:8–9

greatest gift I could give you..." Every good and perfect gift that's been added to my life is because of Jesus. He's done things *in* me, *through* me, and *for* me that would otherwise have been impossible. And when I think about Larry writing, "This is the first time you'll see your new name in print..." it truly amazes me. It's like he could see everything I'd ultimately be doing for God and was saying, "God has plans for you..." I don't know if Larry's really of this earth! *I guess that's why I'm certain we'll be meeting someday at the northeast corner of heaven.*

As for our church, the Fellowship of Plano, God has showered us with blessings. Not only do we have a wonderful congregation, we're able to minister without financial pressure. We're fortunate that Larry's business started the church and continues to support our growth. God has truly blessed us in business *and* financially, so that we're able to fully serve Him. We give all the credit to our Lord and Savior, Jesus Christ.

It's Your Turn

If you feel something is missing in your life, *you need Jesus*. He's the only one who can give you the peace you're longing for. He has wonderful plans for you! You don't have to be perfect to love and serve God. Loving the Lord will not take away from your life; it will add many blessings to it! I've heard too many people say, "I just can't go to church right now. My life's in such a mess. When I get it straightened out, I'll come." *They don't understand.* They'll never be able to "straighten out" their mess without supernatural power. God wants us to get in church and begin building a relationship with Him. Then He helps us from there.

Jesus knows your heart. The Bible says He wants you to confess your sins, and by His blood that was shed on the cross, He'll wipe them all away. *He'll forgive you, right now.* It doesn't matter what you've done. No, you'll never be perfect; but you can have a heart for God if you'll invite Jesus into your life. Don't wait any longer to secure your heavenly home. Just bow your head and say this simple prayer:

Dear Jesus, come into my heart and life.
I know that I'm a sinner.
I acknowledge that You died for my sins
*   and were buried in a tomb.*
I believe that You were resurrected on the
*   third day.*
Please come into my heart and save
*   me now.*
I give my life to You.

It's as simple as that! Welcome to the kingdom! Welcome to your new life in Christ.

Does this mean all your struggles will disappear, or that you'll have to be perfect? *No*, but as a child of God, the Holy Spirit has moved into your life! You'll become more convicted about how you live. You'll have a love for the Lord like none other, and find that you're happiest while growing to know Him and learning how to serve Him. You'll begin to talk to Him and listen to what He desires for you and your life. And you'll want to read His life instruction manual to us, *the Bible*. Oh, what peace, joy, and contentment you can find in Him!

Remember, *it's your choice.* And for me, it's the best choice I've ever made!

Reflections

1. Do you believe all things happen for a reason?

2. Romans 8:28 is an awesome scripture. What do you believe it means? How could it help your life or situation?

3. Sometimes the issues you overcome are still felt by others. For example, forgiveness issues within my family caused difficult situations for me until my biological mother died. If you've experienced similar situations, that possibly caused misunderstandings between family members, how could you bring them to terms?

4. Re-read Matthew 6:25–33 in its entirety. Reflect on your life thus far in light of my story. Has it helped you to develop a "heavenly perspective" about your journey? Go back and read your notes from the *Reflections*; do so on a regular basis. Add more notes as you continue your journey with God. I guarantee you'll gain a new perspective.

5. A lot of people say they're searching for God. Something seems to be missing within their soul; it's the hole that can only be filled by Jesus Christ. Can you or someone you know relate to this? You don't need to search any longer. God knows you and loves you deeply. He wants you to invite Him into your heart. He longs to be close to you and is offering you the free gift of salvation. You don't have to work for it (or earn it). *Just accept it.* I promise that hole will be filled...*for eternity.*

Part III

Things I've Learned "Here" and "There"

...Observe how the lilies of the field grow...even Solomon in all his glory did not clothe himself like one of these.

Matthew 6:28–29

Chapter 12

What Dreams Are Made Of

Life Lessons on Attitude, Family, Money, Weight & More

Did you know the onion species is actually a subfamily of the lily? There are countless varieties of plants that are part of this big family—*literally thousands*. Imagine the implications, then, when Jesus said, "...Observe how the lilies of the field grow..." (Matt. 6:28). It would take a lifetime!

There are over 160 types of lilies found in *American* trade alone![1] This means our choices are virtually unlimited. Isn't that what life is all about? Here we are, back where we started. *Life is made up of choices*. Every choice represents a layer that constitutes who you are; and every day, your choices shape your future. Some choices are easy, and others aren't. That's why some layers of the onion are healthy and others need care.

We have to "observe" the layers; peel back each one, to deal with the issues of our lives. After peeling each layer, we finally get to the center of the onion. *In life, that's when you've reached the heart of the matter.* That's when you've discovered what dreams are made of; when you've learned what matter's most.

On the following pages, I've put together topical reflections drawn from the lessons I've learned in my life. Hopefully, some of these principles will be helpful to you. Read them at your leisure. Reflect on your life. Deal with an unresolved issue. Laugh at a funny anecdote. Cry with a friend.

Most of all, enjoy your life and choose happiness in everything you do! Cherish what God has given you. As you follow Him, He has a wonderful future in store for you.

Age

It's inevitable. Chances are, you wouldn't trade your age for anything, because of everything you've learned and experienced. There's a certain amount of wisdom that comes only with age. Celebrate your life experiences and be the best you can be *right now.*

Numerous surveys have been conducted with the elderly, asking, "What is your one regret?" Overwhelmingly, the answer always seems to be, "I didn't do some things that I really wanted to do." Don't have these same regrets. Consider this moment like you would halftime at the Super Bowl. How do you want the second half to go? Find out what you really want to do in life, and make every effort to reach your goal.

All things are possible with God! Even when you don't believe in yourself, always remember that God does.

Aging

There are two things I've learned about getting older. First, start thinking about taking good care of yourself. Be careful about what you eat, and what you do (this is becoming very real to me!). Second, keep in touch with friends and family.

Our families matter. Remember, it's not about *Me, Me, Me* anymore! This selfish stage generally tends to go away with your twenties and thirties. When you reach your forties, you start thinking, "There are other people out there!"

Certainly, after becoming a Christian you start learning that serving others is the best thing to do. That means building relationships. I haven't always been good at this, so I always strive to do better.

Attitude

Many of us have heard that ten percent of life is about what happens to us, and ninety percent is how we respond. Attitude is everything. It's a matter of perspective. What would your life be like if you thought this way—

Every day is a holiday.
Every meal is a feast.
Every traffic jam is a parade.

Think about it. Is your problem a crisis, or an opportunity? You have the power to decide.

Change

You can't change others—*and this will shock you*—you can't change yourself. Only the Holy Spirit of God can change you. Pray for His guidance and strength, and know that all things are possible through our Almighty God!

If you try to tell others how their lives can be better, they'll end up resenting you. The best thing you can do is to prayerfully improve *your* life and be a good example. People are greatly influenced by what they see *in you*. So put on the mind of Christ everyday. Let your light shine.

Character

Simply put, do what you say you're going to do. It says a lot about you.

Christian Life

Receiving salvation is only the beginning. You'll be happiest in your Christian life when you begin serving God.

Communication

Learn to talk; confront, if you will—not in a bad way, but in a way that says exactly what you want to say. If you hold things in, you'll only grow to resent the other person. And if the resentment builds long enough, it will be almost impossible to recover. Convey your thoughts, needs, and desires: but keep it *relevant*. In other words, stay focused on the issue at hand. In an argument or fight, don't attack the other person's character, and be willing to arrive at a solution. Be willing to listen to your partner (or friend) and try to see things from his or her perspective. Check your pride at the door!

In all communication, be honest, concise, and think things through completely before talking. Say what you mean and mean what you say.

Confidence

Three words: ACT AS IF. There are areas in all of our lives that make us feel less confident. Act as if you're confident, and you'll be amazed at the results. Believe that you're already what you desire to be. Believe in your talents and abilities. If you "act as if" long enough, you may just succeed.

Dating

You have a lot of influence over your choice of people to date. Hang out in a bar, you'll attract others hanging out in bars. Hang out in a circus, you might attract a trainer. Hang out in a hospital, you may attract a doctor. Hang out in a church, or with other Christians, and you may attract someone who loves the Lord. Know you have more control than you think regarding the person you may fall in love with. Believe in yourself *and* your worth. Set your standards high.

Family

I've often wondered why high school kids place so much emphasis on friends. More often than not, you'll never see those people again (except at high school reunions)—and then, who cares? People are already wrapped up in their own, busy lives.

Family, on the other hand, is important. They'll be with you for life. Here are a few important things to remember:

Love your family.
Pray for your family.
Stay in touch as much as possible.
Don't loan money to your family.
Don't mix family and business.

Fear

We Fear
1) What We Don't Understand
2) What We Can't Control

Fear is at the core of a lot of misery in our lives: fear of rejection, failure, dying...the list goes on and on. To get to the heart of an issue, I often use the "Five 'Why' Theory." When someone comes to me with a problem, I keep asking "why," and by the time I get to the fifth "why," I'm starting to find out what the real problem is—and it almost always relates to fear.

Again, it's like peeling layers of an onion. After several layers have been peeled away, you find out what's really bothering that person. The Bible makes many references to fear and tells us not to be afraid. The antidote to fear is FAITH. Understand that God loves you deeply and doesn't wish harm on anyone.

Remember Jeremiah 29:11, "For I know the plans I have for you," declares the LORD, "plans to prosper you and not to harm you, plans to give you hope and a future" (NIV). Psalm 34:4 is another great verse. It says, "I sought the LORD, and He answered me, and delivered me from all my fears."

On the lighter side, talk show host Steve Allen had a guest on his show that said, "My two greatest fears are fear of falling and fear of loud noises." Without skipping a beat, Steve replied, "Yeah, I have the fear of making a loud noise when falling."

Fear comes from our need to do this. Overcome your need to do this. Go to God for help. Admit you're powerless on your own, let go, and let God handle it.

Forgiveness

We Must Learn To Forgive
1) Other People
2) Ourselves

The whole concept of Christianity is, "I'm not perfect, I'm forgiven." God doesn't hold our mistakes against us, *we do*. We live with immeasurable guilt, because we often find it hard to forgive ourselves. Remember, feeling guilty isn't necessarily a bad thing; it actually says you're a decent person! Don't resist the process, ride through it.

Understand what you *can* and *can't* control. You have absolute control over *this moment!* Go to God for help. Pray that He'll heal your heart and the hearts of others toward you.

Hearing about how other people have learned to forgive can be quite healing. For example, some television shows have aired powerful stories about forgiveness. I've seen programs where somebody was able to forgive another person that had murdered their child or family member. You may wonder how that's possible, but here's what I've come to understand.

People can reach a point of desperation where the only way they can live another day is to forgive. When they do, a tremendous weight is lifted. Forgiving others releases those who forgive, filling them with a sense of peace that's often difficult to articulate. Philippians 4:7 says, God gives us peace that *passes all understanding* as we bring everything to Him (RSV).

The Bible is clear that we must forgive others if we want God to forgive us. Matthew 6:14–15 says, "For if you forgive men when they sin against you, your heavenly Father will also forgive you. But if you do not forgive men their sins, your Father will not forgive your sins" (NIV). Forgiveness doesn't mean forgetting. It transcends the event.

Friendship

The best way to lose friends is to always talk about *you*. The best way to gain friends is to talk about them! Surround yourself with:

1. People who are more knowledgeable than you. Don't be intimidated by them. Learn from them.

2. People who lift you up, not bring you down.

3. People who inspire you, encourage you, and make you want to be a better person.

Jack Nicholson told Helen Hunt in the movie, *As Good As It Gets*, "You make me want to be a better man." What a great compliment! As Dr. Phil puts it, there are *contaminators* and *contributors* to every relationship. Be a contributor and hang around with other contributors.

Throughout your life, you'll have many friends. There are three types:

1. Reasonal
2. Seasonal
3. Lifelong

Reasonal friends are people that come into your life for a *reason*. For example, maybe you have a flat tire on the side of the road, and somebody stops to help you. There's a reason that person stops—*so they could help you!* More than likely, you'll never see that person again. One of the reasons God brought Larry into my life at the time He did was to lead me to Him, so that I could begin my spiritual walk (but he also falls into the lifelong category).

Seasonal friends are with you during *certain seasons* of your life. For example, I'm in the early season of motherhood, so I've been developing friendships with other mothers of younger children (so that our kids can play together). If you're single (or maybe a couple with no children), you tend to gravitate toward the same types of people...because it's a season in your life. I've heard about single people who get married, and then try to keep up with their single lives and friends. It usually doesn't work out, because their season has changed.

I've heard lifelong friends can be counted on one hand (I saw on Oprah once that it's usually about two). It's sad, but true! I've had all kinds of friends, but very few have been lifelong. These are the people that stick with you, no matter what. They have their own things going on, but if you call them at 2:00 in the morning saying, "I need you," they'll be there for you.

Giving Thanks

I've heard it takes twenty-one days to make or break a habit. Get in the habit of saying *thanks* to our Lord! If you get in the habit of giving thanks when things are good, you're more likely to give thanks during the bad times (because of the habit you've formed). First Thessalonians 5:18 says, "No matter what happens, always be thankful, for this is God's will for you who belong to Christ Jesus" (TLB).

Happiness and Joyfulness

Here are a few happy thoughts. In her book, *Leaking Laffs between Pampers and Depends*, Barbara Johnson says, "PURITANISM is the haunting fear that someone, somewhere, may be happy.[2]

> Happiness is a talent. ACT as if you have this talent!
> Happiness and being joyful are extremely contagious. Try it!"

Knowledge versus Wisdom

> *"The fear of the LORD is the beginning of wisdom;*
> *all who follow his precepts have good understanding.*
> *To him belongs eternal praise."*
> Ps. 111:10, LAB

Knowledge and wisdom are two different things. The Bible says time and again, we must choose wisdom. Wisdom is the capacity to make good use of knowledge. It's an ability to recognize the difference between right and wrong, and exercise good judgment.

Too much knowledge can be dangerous. It can cause you to want an answer for everything, just to prove things. You can even begin to question your beliefs, because you're filling your head with too much stuff! It may be hard for you to have faith, because you believe there should be an answer for everything. The Bible says, "Now faith is the substance of things hoped for, the evidence of things not seen" (Heb. 11:1, NKJ). We're not supposed to have all the answers, *only God does*. We are to choose wisdom in all that we do.

Let me illustrate. Oftentimes, knowledge isn't enough. We know seatbelts save lives, but do we always wear them? Wisdom comes in wearing one. Do we have knowledge that drinking and driving is a dangerous combination? Yet many people still do it. Do we know that cigarette smoking can cause lung cancer? Yes, but millions of Americans still smoke.

You must have a *plan* to make the best of what you know. Knowledge isn't enough. *Choose wisdom.*

Leadership

Be willing to let go of control. Help others to develop their talents and abilities. It may take some work, but everyone is good at *something*. Look for these things in others, and take the time to develop people! You must be willing to delegate and fully trust that a person can accomplish a task or goal. The biggest pitfalls to effective leadership are:

Delegating the right task to the wrong person.
Delegating the wrong task to the right person.

Find the perfect fit (i.e., the right task for the right person); but when you do, let go of everything and let the person do it. Trust in your decision *and the person* to see it through. If all goes well, celebrate your success. If it doesn't, learn from it and try again—but always acknowledge the value in people.

In a sense, we shy away from letting people develop because we don't want to set them up to fail. This can be dangerous. They'll never realize their full potential unless you challenge them with opportunity.

Timing must also match with the person and the task. Balancing all three elements is essential to becoming a good leader.

Remember, as a leader, everyone won't like you. I can easily think of several ways I could unintentionally offend someone. You'll never please all of the people all the time. However, if you make the best decision in the interest of everyone you're responsible for, ultimately, people will learn to respect your leadership.

Left Hand Column/Right Hand Column Thinking

"A wise man's heart {directs him} toward the right,
but the foolish man's heart {directs him}
toward the left."
Eccl. 10:2

This is a term we used while I was a Corporate Trainer at Southwest Airlines. The Left Hand Column is *what you're thinking.* The Right Hand Column is *what you say.* For instance; someone says to you, "Are you feeling okay?" Automatically, you think, "Oh I must look bad," but that's not what you say. So you say one thing, but think another.

Let me illustrate. If you tell someone whose shoe isn't untied, "Your shoe's untied," they'll probably say, "No, it's not." If you say, "Yes, it is," they'll say it again, "No, it's not." In reality, they're thinking, "Are you crazy? What are you, blind?"—but the whole time, they were being polite. I'm not saying take the liberty to say *whatever* you want *whenever* you want, because you don't want to go around making enemies. Do, however, try to be more honest with others...tactfully.

Honesty is the best policy, because if you lie, you have to remember the lie (and if you don't, you're busted!). When you lie, you usually have to cover it up with even more lies—then you have to remember everything you've said! You can't do it; the burden is much too heavy. And, God doesn't like it.

Try finding a happy medium between Left Hand Column and Right Hand Column thinking.

Listening

Really listen to people. Don't just hear them talk, but really listen to what they're saying. Oftentimes when someone's talking to us, we're daydreaming; because they're talking about something we're simply not interested in. In most cases, we're already formulating our response to what little we've heard them say (or simply want to share what *we* want to share), before they've even finished. So have we really heard them?

Listen intently until they've finished speaking, and then respond. Looking directly into their eyes is very important. In doing this, you're letting them know you value what they're saying. Therefore, you value them as people. This works for everyone!

For goodness' sake, do everything you can to remember *everyone's* name. This includes your college professor *and* the lady who cleans the University. This reminds me of a scene in the movie, *An American President*. The President is getting ready for a date with a lobbyist and his daughter says, "Be sure to compliment her shoes; women like that." People love when you remember...*especially* their names.

Listening To Parents

If you're a young woman or man making a big decision, think about talking to your parents. Believe it or not, they're a lot wiser than you right now. You don't like to admit it. Even though you know more *now* than before, your parents are still much wiser. They've been there, done that. Usually, their advice is the best route to take. Nothing teaches like experience!

Let's say your parents are advising you to attend college: *just look into it!* You may be in love and can't wait to get married, or you may just want to get out and get your own place...be independent. That's what I did. I ended up getting divorced (which almost anybody at that time could have predicted would happen). High school sweetheart situations usually don't work out.

My high school sweetheart and I bought our first home together. We accumulated some possessions: furniture, televisions, and all kinds of things. When we got divorced (which was traumatic enough, because I wasn't sure how to go about getting the divorce at age twenty-three), we had to sell and split up everything. Then I went to college. I did things backwards, and it was difficult.

Looking back, it was a good experience for me, because it made me grow—but it's probably not the way you want to do it. Go to college first. College is a very admirable goal. An undergraduate degree hardly gets you anywhere these days. You almost need a post-graduate, or even doctorate degree to get a good position, so college is extremely important. Even if you're a dream chaser, or want to be an entrepreneur someday, the investment in some college won't hurt.

Look at your options. In the end, you're going to do what *you* want to do—just be aware there may be somebody out there that's a little wiser than you. Don't assume you have all the answers.

Living

Five Ways to Success in Your Christian Life

1. Overcome discouragement.
   - Get a personal relationship with the Lord.
   - Get over the *Me, Me, Me* syndrome. Begin serving others.

2. Get along with others.
   - Spend time with people who pick you up, instead of pulling you down.
   - Spend time with others who know the Lord.

3. Get the right attitude.
   - You have the ability to make that choice.

4. Have a vision for your life.
   - Learn what builds your confidence and take advantage of it!
   - Have a plan and don't be discouraged if it doesn't work. Just try another plan.

5. Get started!
   - Growth sometimes comes little by little. Have patience.
   - There's always something new you can learn.

Marriage

There are countless books on marriage; step-by-step guides on everything from sex to fighting fair—but I've learned a very important key to making your relationship thrive. Every day, ask your spouse, "What can I do for you today?" You'll be amazed at the positive changes that will take place. Love is spelled G I V E.

Money

Feel free to *give* money to someone, but never expect it to be repaid. Larry shared with me once there are three reasons you should never loan money:

1. It's a temporary fix.
2. You're playing God in their lives.
3. They'll resent you for it.

Never use a credit card! If you must, have *one* and pay off the entire amount when the bill arrives. If you're not able to do this, save up for the item you want and pay in cash. There are only two things you should finance:

1. Your home
2. Your car

Credit card debt is a deadly trap. People spend their lives trying to get out of debt, and many never do. In one day, I received six invitations to get a credit card with anywhere from a $2,500–$5,000 limit! And this happens three or four times a week! Also, watch out for the companies that promise financing with no payment for six months. By the time interest charges roll around, it's usually twenty-one percent!

I know a couple that both wanted and needed a car for the past two years. They saved their money and drove an old, used car the whole time until they were able to pay $14,000 in cash for a new one! If only more people were willing to sacrifice like this!

Living beyond your means is dangerous. I recently heard that fifty percent of people living in Plano, Texas (an upscale suburb of Dallas) couldn't furnish the second story of their homes! Why do people do this? Buy a home that you'll be able to furnish. Keeping up with the Jones' will only bring you financial and emotional despair.

Money isn't everything, but it's nice to have. Keep a careful perspective and plan for the future. There will come a time when working will not be possible, and the money will run out. Pray for freedom from financial burdens and secure everything you can to make it happen. With the future being as uncertain as it is now, *it's crucial.*

Overcoming Discouragement

Quit serving yourself—start serving others. You'd be amazed at the joy and peacefulness you feel when you begin to think of others. Your life will be transformed! Remember three things:

1. When you die, you'll be forgotten unless you've made a mark.
2. God forgives all.
3. You can't saw sawdust.

We hear about movie stars dying every day, and then forget. How many times can you remember saying, "I didn't know such-and-so died!" People are forgotten unless they make a mark.

What's the best way to impact someone's life? Let me tell you what a minister friend said about a man named Charlie. Charlie grew up in a small town and drove the bus for his church. He and his family lived in a very modest home out in the middle of nowhere. One day, Charlie showed up at our friend's door, and invited them to church; eventually, they went. At this revival, each of his family members got saved, one by one.

Two years later, our friend's father died...and soon after that, his sister passed away. The only way the family could get through it was by remembering what Charlie had done in bringing them to the Lord. Thank goodness for Charlie! Now our friend's sister and father are in heaven.

Later, this minister told of how he'd been incarcerated and spent five years in prison. Every day he thought of Charlie, and how one day he'd get out and tell him that God had made all the difference in his life. He was able to share God's Word and witness to people in prison. It was so heartwarming!

Charlie's probably gone now, but he made a mark on a lot of people's lives by leading one family to the Lord. He was a bus driver, but he made a mark for many years to come.

If you're discouraged, remember this: *you can't saw sawdust.* It's already dead and gone. A wise preacher friend of mine said: "Your past is the past. Nothing can be different, except from this moment on. You have the ability to change the *now*."

Parenting – General

There are a lot of rules and guidelines for raising children. The bottom line is: You're the parent. You have gut instinct. God has entrusted you with His precious gift. Pray for His guidance and don't succumb to worldly pressures that tell you, 1) How long you should breastfeed, 2) When your child needs to be off of the bottle or pacifier (incidentally, "sucking" is a normal, healthy function of child development. if it's not a "paci," then it will be fingers or a thumb), and 3) When your child should be potty-trained (I haven't seen a lot of school-aged children in diapers!). Get my point?

Raising boys is different than raising girls. Dr. James Dobson has an excellent book entitled, *Bringing Up Boys*, in which he clearly points out that we want our boys to grow into **men**. In his study of homosexuals (and he's encountered hundreds), there was a common denominator in every situation—no dominant male figure in their lives growing up.

Boys need to explore, hunt, and risk a little bit. This is hard for a mom. We want to run to them every time they scrape a knee. It's my job to nurture and love Luke (as his mother), and it's Larry's job to show him fishing, hunting, working a farm, and spitting. This keeps me in perspective.

People will always have an opinion about how you should be raising your child. Filter the advice, use what you can, and thank them for their observations. But most importantly, go with what you feel. God will guide you. Proverbs 22:6 says, "Train up a child in the way he should go, even when he is old he will not depart from it." Take your child to church regularly, pray with him everyday, and always be an excellent example. He has a mental camera, and is taking snapshots of what you say and do all the time.

Moms, we can never love our children enough, and we'll be their biggest influence in life. Think of all the football players that say, "Hi Mom," as soon as the camera points to them! The famous basketball player, Charles Barkley, recently said his biggest inspirations are his mother and grandmother (interestingly, his grandmother is strong and independent, and his mother is very nurturing).

Parenting – Teens and Peer Pressure

If you have a teen or pre-teen (that's gone through abandonment like I did early in life), realize that it's *traumatic*. There's a lasting effect, so you'll have to be careful. I think being super-strict and putting limits on things can be counterproductive (though I understand as a parent, you must have limits, guidelines, and discipline). For instance, my mom wouldn't let me wear jeans to school...I don't really think that's important, but it was a big deal to her.

I think the little things don't matter in life. Try to give your children some space. Let them be creative, empower them, give them responsibility, encourage their talents and abilities, and tell them they can do anything they want in life. I've started that early with Luke, and just the other day, I caught him drawing on the wall and said, "Luke, don't do that!" He replied, "Mommy, you said I can do anything I want to do!"

I also think sometimes you have to let go and let your children be in the crowd to the extent they can relate to their peers—not stand out like a sore thumb. Kids are getting too much pressure. It's hard to be a teen! I believe that's why we've seen so many shooting incidents. Other kids are making fun of them. I guarantee bullying is what causes these kids to go nuts! They get made fun of and teased, and eventually it turns into pure rage. There are facts to support this!

People in General

The bottom line is: *Everyone wants to feel valued.* Find opportunities to see the good in others—we all have good qualities. Recognize these things and tell them, but be specific. Don't just say, "You're wonderful," or "You are so creative." Instead say, "You're wonderful for seeing Susan. She needed you in her fight with cancer...you really made a difference when you brought meals to her home..."

Being specific shows that you care enough to notice. "You're so creative with your ideas for our women's group. A book club would certainly help us in our growth. And garage sales, family dinners, and developing a church cookbook would help us to raise money for the special events we've planned. Thank you for your ideas."

People absolutely love this! Get in the habit of writing notes or telling people in person that you appreciate the special qualities they possess.

Potential

> *"Do you not know that in a race all the runners compete, but [only] one receives the prize? So run [your race] that you may lay hold [of the prize] and make it yours."*
> 1 Cor. 9:24, Ampl.

In her book, *How To Succeed at Being Yourself*, Joyce Meyer included a great chapter entitled, "Free To Develop Your Potential." In it, she says, "When we are confident and free from tormenting fears, we are able to develop our potential and succeed at being all God intended us to be." She then goes on to say, "...but we cannot develop our potential if we fear failure. We will be so afraid of failing or making mistakes that it would prevent us from stepping out."[3]

We should step out in faith more and believe in ourselves. God has big plans for us, and if we can free ourselves from insecurity, self-doubt, and fear, we can really see things happen. If a plan fails, don't be afraid to reassess and begin a new strategy. After all, I heard that Thomas Edison failed 2,000 times before inventing the light bulb. What would have happened if he quit at 1,998? Try, try, and try again.

Priority in Family

God
Spouse
Children

Priority in Life

God
Family
Friends
Others

Public Speaking

Do you know that public speaking ranks up there with "death" as people's number one fear? One of the scariest things in the world is talking to a room full of people. Why? We're afraid to fail. To some, speaking is a gift; to others, it's not—but anyone can do it. In a speech or talk of any kind, there are three things to remember:

1. Tell'em what you're gonna tell'em.
2. Tell'em.
3. Tell'em what you told'em.

And I always like to add, *just be you*. Nobody does it better!

Relationships

Again, be an example for others. Be what you want others to be, and respect your differences. There's a reason they invented chocolate and vanilla ice cream—not everyone is the same! If we were, the world would be an extremely boring place!

We tend to gravitate to people who are like us (i.e., those who have similar likes and dislikes). We segregate ourselves on a daily basis—which people we'll talk to, eat lunch with, and so on.

Ask yourself which qualities you're looking for in a friend, colleague, or mate; and then ask, "How do I measure up?"

Oftentimes in my relationship with Larry, I've had to learn to be quiet (which is hard for me), and certainly we both readily forgive each other when needed. We love and respect each other deeply.

Obviously, the most important relationship in your life is the one you have with Jesus Christ. Not only does it secure your entry to heaven, it will fill you with peace, hope, happiness, and joy—even when you're walking through difficult times.

Sacrifice

The greatest sacrifice of all happened when Jesus died on the cross for the sins of mankind. Sacrifice is just that, *sacrifice*. *Webster's New World Dictionary of the American Language* defines it as, "The act of giving up, destroying, permitting injury to, or forgoing something valued for the sake of something having a more pressing claim."[4]

If you're not giving up something that's extremely important to you, then it's not a sacrifice. If you're willing to give up driving a new car (until you're able to afford it), then you're sacrificing. If you're willing to give up earning a second income for the family in order to be a stay at home mom, then you're sacrificing. If you start a new business or venture, initially, you'll be sacrificing security, finances, and so on, in order to reap the rewards of a successful business later on.

Sacrifice is undesirable and, at times, can hurt—but some things *must be sacrificed* to reap the future benefits. Fear keeps us from stepping out on faith; but with faith, obedience to God, hard work, and sacrifice, you'll realize plans God has for your life that you never thought were possible.

Self-Image

We all want to belong, feel worthwhile, and be capable. God wants to use us in ways we never thought possible—and we've been created in His image! It just doesn't get any better than that. Above all, we should recognize ourselves as children of the King. We have royal blood running through our veins. We're His sons and daughters, not cousins or grandchildren, but sons and daughters.

If we're too consumed with an image we're trying to project to the world, it will be difficult for God to use us. The world will give you a poor self-image. Just look at television, movies, and magazines! Women are all portrayed as flawless, and a size two. If we look on worldly things, it can definitely affect our self-perception.

Remember Matthew 6:33, "But seek first His kingdom and His righteousness..." James 4:4 adds, "...don't you know that friendship with the world is hatred toward God? Anyone who chooses to be a friend of the world becomes an enemy of God" (NIV). Don't look to the world, but focus on Him! God sees you as being beautiful and fully capable.

Sex

Never use as a reward or punishment. It's a beautiful, God-given act between a husband and wife. Be attentive to your spouse, make time for one another. Get creative, communicate constantly, and enjoy your mate.

Skin Care

I made some bad mistakes caring for my skin when I was younger that are just starting to show up now in the form of age spots (from what I've read, this comes from damage sustained up to twenty-five years ago, and the more I think about it, the more it makes sense).

I've always had great skin, and was always quick to tan. When I was a young girl, I never thought twice about rubbing baby oil on my skin and laying on the roof of my parent's house. Then when I graduated from high school and left home, I went to Corpus Christi with seven girlfriends and we all decided we weren't going to use sun block—and we were there for about five days! I got severely burned. Eventually, I got blisters all over my body.

Keith (my fiancé at the time) called and asked different people we knew for advice. I think he even called the doctor and asked, "What can I do for her?" One person apparently told him to crack eggs into a bath for me so they'd ooze on my skin. So we bought a couple dozen eggs, put them in the bath...and it didn't help. We tried aloe baths and all kinds of remedies. It was awful. I was miserable.

I still don't know why I didn't go to the Emergency Room, because the burns were certainly bad enough. I could only sleep in certain positions, and only on the sheets. All the blankets had to be thrown off. *I never tanned without sun block again.*

If you're young, take care of your skin. You'll definitely appreciate it when you get older—because the damage that happens now won't show up for many years. Don't make the mistake of thinking you're invincible. Be smart now for later.

Stress

There's good stress and bad stress. Good stress is your wedding day, or the day you become a parent. Bad stress is your marriage and being a parent! *Just kidding.*

Stress comes in many forms, and is the cause of numerous health problems today. Stress is physically and emotionally draining. Bad stress can come from discontentment because of unrealistic expectations: an image of what your life *should look like* instead of what it is.

Don't put your life on hold because of some idealized image of what it should be. The movie, *It's A Wonderful Life,* comes to mind. If you're sick, Christmas won't cure it. (We often dread the holidays, because our inner experience is so different than the hype. The same is true throughout the year.) Be realistic.

Success

My cousin, Jack Butler, told me, "Success is very simple:

> Do what you say you're going to do...
> When you say you're going to do it...
> At the price you agreed upon."

Remember Matthew 5:37, "Simply let your 'Yes' be 'Yes,' and your 'No,' 'No'; anything beyond this comes from the evil one" (NIV).

Teaching

Repetition increases retention. Don't be afraid to make the same points several times. Reiterating information helps people to remember.

If you're using teaching aids like flow charts and overhead projectors, don't worry so much about the spelling of your words. Larry has always told me, and I agree, "I've never respected anyone that can't spell the same word four or five different ways!"

Instead of telling people how to do something, let them do it. If you've never made a pot of coffee, I could tell you how to do it ten times, but when you actually make a pot for yourself, then you've learned!

Time Management

How you spend your time has everything to do with what you deem to be important at that very moment. Enough said.

The Opposite Sex

There are countless books about the differences between men and women. Face it, we're different. God made us that way. Learn what you can about these differences, but don't go into a frenzy because you can't fully understand your spouse. You probably never will...but you can find peace.

A man's greatest fear is failure: Failure to provide for his family, or to perform, or measure up.

A woman's greatest fear is that she won't be loved or desired.

Instead of criticizing a man about who he isn't, try telling him how much you appreciate who he is. You'll find the more you lift him up and have faith in him, the more he'll want to perform for your family. The same thing is true for a woman. The more you tell her how desirable she is and how much you love her, the more she'll want to perform for you.

Face it. Don't you want to do more things for someone that makes you feel good about yourself?

Weight

As you get older, you start thinking, "I need to eat better. I need to quit shoving in the sugar and think about maybe putting in some vegetables..." Lately, I've been thinking a lot more about my weight and preparing my eating habits and weight for what I want them to be in my fifties and sixties.

I don't want to be skinny as I get older, because I think God puts a little extra weight on you to protect you during menopause, or against osteoporosis. I believe there's a reason why a lot of women gain about 10–15 pounds that they just can't take off. This could be God's way of saying, "No, I want you to have it..." Still, we need to be very cognizant of what we eat and how we maintain our weight.

I remember being a tall, lanky child all of my life. Tall and skinny. When I was sixteen or seventeen, my family took a vacation to Monterey, Mexico. In those pictures, my two younger sisters are tiny and I'm towering above them—tall, thin, and no waist! I definitely had a boyish figure.

I have a tremendous sweet tooth, and around that time of my life, I was sneaking to the gas station/convenience store about two miles down the road on my bike. It could have been summertime and I'd wear a coat, knowing that I was going to the store to get Snowballs, Swiss Cake Rolls and Twinkies! I'd say, "Bye, I'm going out bike riding." I'd buy a coat full of them, and stick them in all the pockets. Then I'd come back home and shove them in my drawers.

Mom was really good about not keeping sweets in the house. She'd keep some, but not a whole lot, because *she knew*. And she wouldn't let us drink coke; we always had to drink juice, or something else healthy. I longed for cokes and sweets, so I'd get them for myself, store them in my room, and eat them all week. I was so skinny, I didn't have to worry about it.

When I graduated from high school, I took a job at an insurance company. I ate and ate, but I stayed skinny. I was looking good. Then I went to work for the bank and did the same thing. By then, I was about twenty-three. I remember one day asking a couple of my friends, "Do you have any clothes that you could let me wear?" because they were bigger than I was. "I think I need a bigger size pants," I said. One of the girls said she had some clothes that she could give me. She'd noticed that I'd gained weight.

I remember putting on the larger garments thinking, "Well, I'm just a little bigger, but it's not bad." The weight just crept up on me, and I didn't even notice it until my friend asked, "Barb, aren't you a little concerned?" At that moment, I thought, "Oh, well, maybe I don't need to weigh this much." That's when I started thinking about weight. I guess I'd be 400 pounds by now if she hadn't said anything!

I've been on everything imaginable as far as diets, but I've learned that *eating less* and *exercising more* is the ticket. Diets are too restrictive. You want things that you can't have, so when you come off of the diet, you gain the weight back (and possibly more).

I've really been trying to balance eating and exercise...but I refuse to beat myself up about it. I'm just trying to be consistent. So make good food choices when you can, and do a little bit of exercise regularly. Make it a habit, something you'll eventually not have to think too much about—like brushing your teeth every morning. Moderation and consistency are what's most important.

---

[1] Encyclopedia.com. "Lily: Economic Importance."
[2] Johnson, Barbara. *Leaking Laffs between Pampers and Depends*, p. 55. Word Publishing, a Thomas Nelson Company, Nashville, TN. Copyright © 2000 by Barbara Johnson.
[3] Meyer, Joyce. *How To Succeed at Being Yourself*, p. 77. Harrison House, Inc. Tulsa, OK 74153. Copyright © 1999 by Joyce Meyer.
[4] Guralnik, David B., Editor in Chief. *Webster's New World Dictionary of the American Language*, p. 1252. Simon and Schuster. New York, NY 10020. Copyright © 1982.

Reflections

1. What's the one thing you know for sure?

Uncertain About Tomorrow? We Have Good News Today!

We've been waiting for you! And we're excited to share with you the marvelous ways God is working in our church.

It won't take you long to discover this is truly a family, rich in relationships that matter most. Growing together, we worship, serve, laugh, cry, learn, and reach out to our world with life-transforming truth.

We're eager to know you.

Pastor Larry and Barb

- **Relaxed, Casual Atmosphere**
- **Practical Messages that Relate to Your Life**
- **Children's and Youth Activities**
- **Great Events, Retreats, and Fellowship**
- **Loving Nursery Care**

Sunday Worship Celebration
and Children's Church
10:30 a.m.
(Sunday School at 9:30 a.m.)

Wednesday Worship Service
Praise Kids and Youth Groups
6:45 p.m.
(Fellowship Dinner at 6:00 p.m.)

Reel to Real—For Women
Bible Group
Tuesday at 9:30 a.m.
Every First Tuesday at 7:00 p.m.
(Summer Meetings, ONLY First Tuesday p.m.)

FELLOWSHIP
OF PLANO

6700 Independence Parkway
Plano, TX 75023
972.618.8237 Office
972.208.1608 Fax
fop@airmail.net

Our Mission
Is To Be A Church That...

Exalts the Savior
Emphasizes the Scripture
Empowers the Individual
Encourages the Family
Equips the Church
Evangelizes the World
Expects the Impossible!

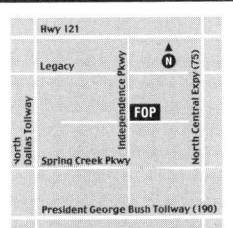

Come As You Are!

Barbara Butler Norrell
Author, Publisher, and Motivational Speaker

A Few Great *Reel to Real* Teaching Series

"Beauty and The Beast"
Identifying How Satan Plays on Fear and Disguises Himself as Beautiful

"Bounce"
Steps to Forgiveness

"The Legend of Bagger Vance"
Freedom from Emotional Pain

Call LARA for a full product listing today!

"Titanic"
A Voyage without God

"The Story of Us"
Understanding the Differences between Men and Women

Available on Audio and Video through LARA Publishing

Contact Barb
& Her Team
at LARA
to Speak at Your
Church
Organization
Meeting
or Special Event!

➡ Services Currently Available
Motivational Speaker & Bible Teacher
Conference & Seminar Host

Ministry Leader
Co-Founder, Fellowship of Plano
Founder, *Reel to Real* Bible Study for Women
Co-Founder, *Women of Strength*

Business Owner/Entrepreneur
Founder, LARA Enterprises
Founder, SNBT Sales

Corporate Professional
Financial Analyst & Trainer, Southwest Airlines
Previously Certified through Southwest:
- Frontline Leadership Trainer
- Challenge (Ropes) Course Facilitator
- Franklin Time Management Instructor

Featured Speaker, "Real Time" Management/
Louisiana Baptist University

Contact LARA Publishing Today!
For Bookings, Products, and More Information
972.429.5185 • **972.429.5935** Fax
bnorrellnow@yahoo.com

Ratzinger 17, 19, 191, 204, 205, 212
Roman Catholic 7, 10, 161, 179, 180, 181, 186, 187, 188, 189

S

Schillebeeckx, Edward 125, 210
Schweitzer, Albert 14, 204
sect 16, 18, 24, 33, 34, 51, 87, 95, 96, 97, 102, 110, 112, 151, 167
Septuagint 30, 114, 118
Siricius 102, 104, 117, 162
social construction of reality 25, 35, 77
Soter 99, 104
Stark, Rodney 52, 69, 70, 71, 72, 83, 208
Stephen I, bishop 100
Stephen, martyr 101
Sylvester, bishop of Rome 101, 102, 104, 137, 140
synoptic problem 55, 56

T

Talpiot 176, 177
technology 35
Thecla 48, 49, 50, 207
Titus, arch of 67
Trajan 16, 73, 81
Trypho 91
two source hypothesis 56

U

Urban I 100, 104

V

Valentinus 107, 109
Victor I 99, 104

W

White, Michael 42, 61, 75, 105, 108, 204, 206, 208
Wills, Garry 51, 158, 159, 185, 206, 207, 208, 212
women 9, 11, 12, 19, 21, 22, 27, 30, 31, 40, 41, 42, 43, 44, 46, 47, 48, 49, 50, 51, 52, 58, 59, 61, 62, 64, 66, 68, 69, 74, 76, 78, 85, 96, 107, 110, 111, 112, 115, 120, 122, 123, 124, 125, 126, 127, 136, 143, 146, 156, 159, 160, 167, 168, 172, 187, 188, 191, 194, 196, 207

Z

Zosimus 68, 163, 164, 197, 212

Printed in the United Kingdom
by Lightning Source UK Ltd.
136058UK00002B/75/P